Cambridge Essentials

Mathematics

Fiona McGill
Ric Pimentel
Peter Ransom
Paul Rigby
Peter Sherran
Rowena Wilcox

Series editors: Graham Newman
Peter Sherran

Extension **8**

CAMBRIDGE
UNIVERSITY PRESS

CAMBRIDGE UNIVERSITY PRESS
Cambridge, New York, Melbourne, Madrid, Cape Town, Singapore,
São Paulo, Delhi, Dubai, Tokyo

Cambridge University Press
The Edinburgh Building, Cambridge CB2 8RU, UK

www.cambridge.org
Information on this title: www.cambridge.org/9780521723817

© Cambridge University Press 2009

First published 2009
Reprinted 2009

Printed in the United Kingdom by Latimer Trend

A catalogue record for this publication is available from the British Library

ISBN 978-0-521-72381-7 Paperback with CD-ROM

Additional resources for this publication at essentials.cambridge.org/mathematics

Contents

Take advantage of the pupil CD

Cambridge Essentials Mathematics comes with a pupil CD in the back. This contains the entire book as an interactive PDF file, which you can read on your computer using free Adobe Reader software from Adobe (www.adobe.com/products/acrobat/readstep2.html). As well as the material you can see in the book, the PDF file gives you extras when you click on the buttons you will see on most pages; see the inside front cover for a brief explanation of these.

To use the CD, simply insert it into the CD or DVD drive of your computer. You will be prompted to install the contents of the CD to your hard drive. Installing will make it easier to use the PDF file, because the installer creates an icon on your desktop that launches the PDF directly. However, it will run just as well straight from the CD.

If you want to install the contents of the disc onto your hard disc yourself, this is easily done. Just open the disc contents in your file manager (for Apple Macs, double click on the CD icon on your desktop; for Windows, open My Computer and double click on your CD drive icon), select all the files and folders and copy them wherever you want.

Take advantage of the teacher CD

The *Teacher Material* CD-ROM for *Cambridge Essentials Mathematics* contains enhanced interactive PDFs. As well as all the features of the pupil PDF, teachers also have access to e-learning materials and links to the *Essentials Mathematics* Planner – a new website with a full lesson planning tool, including worksheets, homeworks, assessment materials and guidance. The e-learning materials are also fully integrated into the Planner, letting you see the animations in context and alongside all the other materials.

Integers

- Multiplying and dividing integers

Keywords

You should know

explanation 1a   explanation 1b

1 Work these out.

  a $4 - 8$ **b** $-9 + 23$ **c** $26 - 32$ **d** $-18 + 36$

  e $14 + 17 - 20$ **f** $-22 - 13 + 16$ **g** $-12 + 15 + 26$ **h** $-32 - 8 + 15$

2 Copy and complete these.

  a $5 + -2 = 5 \square 2 = \square$ **b** $-3 - -7 = -3 \square 7 = \square$

  c $0 - -9 = 0 \square 9 = \square$ **d** $-11 + -12 - -6 = -11 \square 12 \square 6 = \square$

  e $5 + -13 - -7 = 5 \square 13 \square 7 = \square$

  f $14 - -24 + -18 = 14 \square 24 \square 18 = \square$

3 Work these out.

  a $10 - -15$ **b** $-20 - 12$ **c** $40 + -15$

  d $-30 + -10$ **e** $-20 - -15 + 4$ **f** $18 - -22 + -30$

  g $-22 + -4 - -8$ **h** $-26 - -10 + 5$ **i** $-2 + (+5)$

  j $-10 + (-3)$ **k** $1 - (+9) - (-5)$ **l** $-100 - (-8) - 4$

4 Copy and complete the table.

x	18	7	11	3	−4	−7	−12		1	8	−10	−6
y	13	12	−2		−6		−5	−9	−1			4
$x - y$				1		0		4		−2		
$x + y$											−3	

explanation 2

5 Copy and complete these multiplication tables.

   a **i** $3 \times 3 = 9$

           $2 \times 3 = \square$

           $1 \times 3 = 3$

           $0 \times 3 = 0$

           $-1 \times 3 = -3$

           $-2 \times 3 = \square$

           $-3 \times 3 = -9$

   ii $3 \times -3 = -9$

           $2 \times -3 = \square$

           $1 \times -3 = -3$

           $0 \times -3 = \square$

           $-1 \times -3 = \square$

           $-2 \times -3 = 6$

           $-3 \times -3 = \square$

   b Describe the pattern in the answer columns.

   c What do you notice about the answer when a negative number and a positive number are multiplied together?

   d What can you say about the answer when two negative numbers are multiplied together?

6 Work these out.

   a 2×-6 **b** -7×-4 **c** -3×7 **d** 9×-8

   e 5×-12 **f** -8×15 **g** -10×-23 **h** -6×20

   i -16×-4 **j** -100×32 **k** 50×-14 **l** -25×-5

   m $(-4)^2$ **n** $(-1)^2$ **o** $(-7)^2$ **p** $2 \times (-5)^2$

7 Copy and complete this multiplication grid.

$\times$	-2		3	-7
		20		
-9		-45		
			-9	
				-42

8 List all the pairs of integers you can multiply together to give each number.

   a -6 **b** 18   **c** -9

9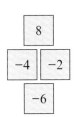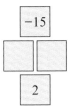

8	−20	−15	24	−20	−4
−4 −2	2 −10				
−6	−8	2	−11	1	0

a What is the link between the two middle numbers and the top number?

b What is the link between the two middle numbers and the bottom number?

c Copy and complete the last four diagrams.

> **explanation 3**

10 a How many times does −3 fit into −12?

  b How many times does −7 fit into −63?

11 Work these out.

a 45 ÷ −5	**b** −36 ÷ −4	**c** −20 ÷ 2	**d** −30 ÷ 6
e 56 ÷ −7	**f** 72 ÷ −8	**g** −60 ÷ 4	**h** −96 ÷ −12
i −120 ÷ −8	**j** 64 ÷ −8	**k** −48 ÷ −3	**l** 100 ÷ −25

12 Using multiplication or division with positive and negative numbers, write four calculations for each of these answers.

  a −16   **b** 32   **c** −42   **d** −60

13 Copy and complete the table.

x	36	−84	−48		72	−65		−17
y	−9	12		−8	−2		13	
$x \div y$			−6	−8		5	−3	−17

14 Work these out.

  a −3 × −8 ÷ 4   **b** 36 ÷ −9 × −2   **c** −70 ÷ −7 × −4.5

  d 16 × −4 ÷ −8   **e** 12 ÷ −6 × −7   **f** −121 ÷ 11 × −7

  g 9 × 7 ÷ −3   **h** −150 × −2 ÷ −30   **i** 25 × −12 ÷ 6

15 a Work out the result of each calculation.

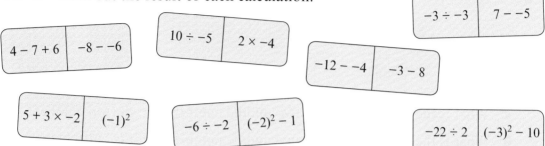

| $4 - 7 + 6$ | $-8 - -6$ |

| $10 \div -5$ | 2×-4 |

| $-3 \div -3$ | $7 - -5$ |

| $-12 - -4$ | $-3 - 8$ |

| $5 + 3 \times -2$ | $(-1)^2$ |

| $-6 \div -2$ | $(-2)^2 - 1$ |

| $-22 \div 2$ | $(-3)^2 - 10$ |

b Arrange the dominos so that ends with the same answer are joined, starting with the double. What is the answer to the part of the last domino that is not joined to another one?

16 Copy and complete the table.

x	-8	-12	7	9	-7	15	-3	-0.5	10	-8
y	-2									
$x + y$										
$x - y$				3						
$x \times y$			-14					1		32
$x \div y$		3		-4.5		-3	0.5		-0.1	

17 a Paula is trying to solve this equation.

$$x^2 - x - 12 = 0$$

The teacher says there are two solutions.

 i Paula tries $x = -5$ first. Explain why this is not a solution to the equation.

 ii Find the two solutions.

b Use a similar method to find the two solutions to these equations.

 i $x^2 + 6x + 5 = 0$

 ii $x^2 + x - 6 = 0$

> Hint: Try the numbers
>
> $-5, -4, -3, -2, -1, 0, 1, 2, 3, 4, 5$
>
> to solve $x^2 - x - 12 = 0$.
>
> Try $x = -5$:
>
> $x^2 - x - 12 = (-5)^2 - -5 - 12$
>
> $\qquad = 25 + 5 - 12$
>
> $\qquad = 18$

Powers and roots

- Cubing positive and negative numbers
- Finding the cube root of a number
- Using power notation

Keywords

You should know

explanation 1a   explanation 1b

1 Fiona thinks 20^2 is 40 and Ben thinks 20^2 is 400. Explain who is right.

2 a Copy and complete the list of square numbers.

$1^2 = 1$	$11^2 =$	$21^2 =$
$2^2 = 4$	$12^2 =$	$22^2 =$
$3^2 = 9$	$13^2 =$	$23^2 =$
$4^2 = 16$	$14^2 =$	$24^2 =$
$5^2 = 25$	$15^2 =$	$25^2 =$
$6^2 = 36$	$16^2 =$	$26^2 =$
$7^2 = 49$	$17^2 =$	$27^2 =$
$8^2 = 64$	$18^2 =$	$28^2 =$
$9^2 = 81$	$19^2 =$	$29^2 =$
$10^2 = 100$	$20^2 =$	$30^2 =$

b The last digit of a number is 0.
What is the last digit of the square of this number?

c If the last digit of a number is 1 or 9, the last digit of the number squared is 1.
Write down four more similar facts by looking at the last digits of the numbers in the list.

d A palindromic number reads the same in reverse, for example 2002.
Write three palindromic square numbers.

e Brian has found two square numbers that add up to another square number.

$3^2 + 4^2 = 5^2$ since $9 + 16 = 25$

Find two more sets of numbers like Brian's.

3 Lagrange (1736–1813) was a famous mathematician who proved that any whole number can be expressed as the sum of four square numbers.

$6 = 2^2 + 1^2 + 1^2 + 0^2$ $\qquad$ $25 = 4^2 + 2^2 + 2^2 + 1^2$

a Write each number as the sum of four square numbers.

$\qquad$ **i** 7 $\qquad$ **ii** 20 $\qquad$ **iii** 100 $\qquad$ **iv** 18 $\qquad$ **v** 35

b The teacher asks the class to write 124 as the sum of four square numbers. Catherine was the first to get an answer. This is her answer.

$$124 = 10^2 + 4^2 + 2^2 + 2^2$$

$\qquad$ **i** Is Catherine's answer right?

$\qquad$ **ii** Other pupils in the class claim that they have different answers that are also correct. Find four other possible answers.

c Write down five different possible ways of expressing 50 as the sum of four square numbers. Here is one to get you started.

$$5^2 + 5^2 + 0^2 + 0^2 = 25 + 25 + 0 + 0 = 50$$

d Repeat part **c** using your own choice of number. Challenge the person sitting next to you to find all your ways.

4 Work these out.

$\qquad$ **a** $\sqrt{16}$ $\qquad$ **b** $\sqrt{49}$ $\qquad$ **c** $\sqrt{25}$ $\qquad$ **d** $\sqrt{100}$

$\qquad$ **e** $\sqrt{144}$ $\qquad$ **f** $\sqrt{100} + \sqrt{49}$ $\qquad$ **g** $\sqrt{196} - \sqrt{64}$ $\qquad$ **h** $\sqrt{81} + \sqrt{25}$

$\qquad$ **i** $3^2 \times \sqrt{121}$ $\qquad$ **j** $\sqrt{169} \times \sqrt{36}$ $\qquad$ **k** $\sqrt{16} \times \sqrt{100}$ $\qquad$ **l** $\sqrt{1600}$

5 Copy and complete these statements.

$\qquad$ **a** $\sqrt{400} = \sqrt{(\square \times 100)} = \sqrt{\square} \times \sqrt{\square} = \square \times 10 = \square$

$\qquad$ **b** $\sqrt{2500} = \sqrt{(\square \times \square)} = \sqrt{\square} \times \sqrt{\square} = \square \times \square = \square$

$\qquad$ **c** $\sqrt{6400} = \sqrt{(\square \times \square)} = \sqrt{\square} \times \sqrt{\square} = \square \times \square = \square$

$\qquad$ **d** $\sqrt{900} = \sqrt{(\square \times \square)} = \sqrt{\square} \times \sqrt{\square} = \square \times \square = \square$

6 $2^2 = 4$. This can be written as the sum of two prime numbers: $2 + 2 = 4$.

$3^2 = 9$. This can also be written as the sum of two prime numbers: $2 + 7 = 9$.

Is it possible to write every square number up to 12^2 as the sum of two prime numbers?

(explanation 2a) (explanation 2b)

7 Here is a sequence of diagrams showing the **cube numbers** 1, 8, 27.

$1^3 = 1 \times 1 \times 1 = 1$ $2^3 = 2 \times 2 \times 2 = 8$ $3^3 = 3 \times 3 \times 3 = 27$

a Copy and complete this table showing the first eighteen cube numbers. You will need a calculator.

n	1	2	3	4	5	6	7	8	9	10	11	12	13	14	15	16	17	18
n^3	1	8	27															

b The number 212 is a palindromic number because it reads the same when the digits are reversed.

Write the palindromic cube numbers from the table.

c $27^3 = 19\,683$ and $1 + 9 + 6 + 8 + 3 = 27$.

Find two other cube numbers from the table with digits that add up to the number that is being cubed.

d Every whole number can be written as the sum of nine or fewer cube numbers.

For example $40 = 3^3 + 2^3 + 1^3 + 1^3 + 1^3 + 1^3 + 1^3$

because $27 + 8 + 1 + 1 + 1 + 1 + 1 = 40$

Write each of these numbers as the sum of cube numbers. Try to use the smallest amount of cube numbers you can.

i 20   **ii** 100   **iii** 19   **iv** 31   **v** 65

e Find a number between 1 and 30 that must be written in this way as the sum of exactly nine cube numbers.

8 a The diagram shows the first five triangular numbers.
Write the next two triangular numbers.

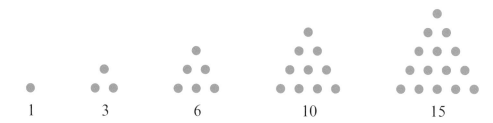

| 1 | 3 | 6 | 10 | 15 |

b Work these out.

i 1^3 **ii** $1^3 + 2^3$ **iii** $1^3 + 2^3 + 3^3$ **iv** $1^3 + 2^3 + 3^3 + 4^3$

c Is there a link between the triangular numbers and the sums of cube numbers?

d Use what you have discovered to explain how you could find the answer to $1^3 + 2^3 + 3^3 + 4^3 + 5^3 + 6^3 + 7^3$.

9 Copy the table and put one number in each space until the table is filled.

3, 4, 8, 9, 12, 16, 25, 27, 64

Use each number once.

	Even	Cube number	Odd
Factors of 24			
Square number			
Multiples of 3			

10 Work these out.

a $\sqrt[3]{1}$ **b** $\sqrt[3]{64}$ **c** $\sqrt[3]{216}$ **d** $3 \times \sqrt[3]{8}$ **e** $\sqrt[3]{27} + \sqrt[3]{64}$

f $2 \times \sqrt[3]{512}$ **g** $\sqrt[3]{1} + \sqrt[3]{343} - \sqrt[3]{125}$ **h** $\sqrt[3]{1000} \times \sqrt[3]{8}$

11 Write each expression using powers. The first one has been completed for you.

a $3 \times 3 \times 3 \times 3 = 3^4$ **b** $7 \times 7 \times 7 \times 7 \times 7$

c $5 \times 5 \times 5 \times 5 \times 5 \times 5 \times 5$ **d** $6 \times 6 \times 6$

e $9 \times 9 \times 9 \times 9 \times 9 \times 9 \times 9 \times 9 \times 9$ **f** $13 \times 13 \times 13 \times 13$

g $10 \times 10 \times 10 \times 10 \times 10$ **h** $10 \times 10 \times 10$

12 The pyramid numbers are 1, 5, 14, 30, …

Notice that

$1 = 1^2$

$5 = 1^2 + 2^2$

$14 = 1^2 + 2^2 + 3^2$

$30 = 1^2 + 2^2 + 3^2 + 4^2$

a Write down the next two numbers in the sequence.

b What will the 10th pyramid number be?

c Why do you think these numbers are called pyramid numbers?

> **explanation 3**

13 Work these out.

a $(-2)^3$ **b** $(-3)^3$ **c** $(-5)^3$ **d** $(-6)^3$ **e** $(-9)^3$

14 The teacher says that the equation

$x^3 - 7x + 6 = 0$

has three integer solutions between −4 and +4.
He asks the class to work out which of
the numbers −4, −3, −2, −1, 0, 1, 2 , 3, 4
are solutions.

$(-3)^3 - 7 \times -3 + 6$

$= -27 - -21 + 6$

$= -27 + 21 + 6$

$= 0$

$3^3 - 7 \times 3 + 6$

$= 27 - 21 + 6$

$= 12$

a Chris tries −3. Is this a solution?

b Tony tries 3. Is this a solution?

c Find the other two solutions.

d Use the same numbers to solve $x^3 - 13x + 12 = 0$.

> **explanation 4**

15 Use a calculator to work these out.

a 18^2 **b** 27^2 **c** 65^2 **d** 81^2

e 120^2 **f** $109^2 - 96^2$ **g** $74^2 + 33^2$ **h** $55^2 - 16^2 - 39^2$

16 Use a calculator to work these out.

   a 2.5^2 **b** 5.8^2 **c** 6.1^2 **d** 8.9^2 **e** 7.3^2 **f** 10.2^2

   g 13^3 **h** 20^3 **i** 16^3 **j** 25^3 **k** 1.8^3 **l** 10.1^3

---

explanation 5

---

17 Complete these statements by finding the two consecutive whole numbers that are on either side of these square roots.

   a $\square < \sqrt{6} < \square$ **b** $\square < \sqrt{24} < \square$ **c** $\square < \sqrt{45} < \square$

   d $\square < \sqrt{88} < \square$ **e** $\square < \sqrt{152} < \square$ **f** $\square < \sqrt{200} < \square$

18 Chi is trying to find x if $x^3 = 5$.

   a Look at Chi's work, explain his strategy.

   b What number should Chi try next?

   c Continue with Chi's table and find the closest numbers with 2 decimal places to complete this statement.

      $\square < x < \square$

x	Working out x^3	Comment
1	$1^3 = 1$	Too small
2	$2^3 = 8$	Too big
1.5	$1.5^3 = 3.375$	Too small
1.7	$1.7^3 = 4.913$	Too small
1.8	$1.8^3 = 5.832$	Too big

19 Phil has a harder equation to solve.

   Find x if $x^3 + x = 3$.

   a How does Phil know the answer lies between 1 and 2?

   b What number should he try next?

   c Find the closest numbers with 2 decimal places to complete the statement $\square < x < \square$.

x	Working out $x^3 + x$	Comment
1	$1^3 + 1 = 2$	Too small
2	$2^3 + 2 = 10$	Too big

20 Use a similar method to find numbers to complete $\square < x < \square$ for the equation $x^3 - x = 50$.

Your numbers should have 2 decimal places.

Multiples, factors and primes

- Finding lowest common multiples
- Finding highest common factors
- Finding prime factors
- Using prime factors to find HCF and LCM

Keywords

You should know

explanation 1

1 a The blue squares are multiples of which number?

b What is the next multiple of this number that is not shown on this 10 by 10 grid?

c The numbers circled in red are the last two multiples of a number on the grid.

What is this number?

d What is the lowest common multiple (LCM) of your answers to parts **a** and **c**?

e What is the smallest common multiple of these two numbers that is not shown on the grid?

1	2	3	4	5	6	7	8	9	10
11	12	13	14	15	16	17	18	19	20
21	22	23	24	25	26	27	28	29	30
31	32	33	34	35	36	37	38	39	40
41	42	43	44	45	46	47	48	49	50
51	52	53	54	55	56	57	58	59	60
61	62	63	64	65	66	67	68	69	70
71	72	73	74	75	76	77	78	79	80
81	82	83	84	85	86	87	88	89	90
91	92	93	94	95	96	97	98	99	100

2 Find the lowest common multiple (LCM) of each set of numbers.

   a 2, 5   **b** 4, 14   **c** 6, 9   **d** 3, 7

   e 12, 15   **f** 3, 5, 6   **g** 4, 10, 12   **h** 5, 8, 10

3 a The LCM of two numbers is 30, what might the numbers be?

   b Find three numbers whose LCM is 36.

explanation 2

4 Write down all the factors of these numbers.

    a 26   **b** 32   **c** 27   **d** 40   **e** 48

5 Sally is placing the factors of 12, 40 and 64 in a diagram.
She starts with the factors of 12.
1 and 2 are factors of all three numbers so she writes 1 and 2 in the area where the three ovals overlap.
3 is a factor of 12 only so she writes 3 in the area for factors of 12 only.

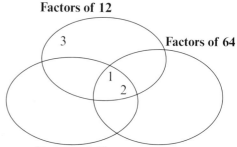

    a Copy and complete the diagram by placing all the factors of 12, 40 and 64 in the correct place.

    b What are the common factors of 12, 40 and 64?

    c What is the highest common factor of 12, 40 and 64?

    d Find the common factors and highest common factors of each set of numbers.

      i 30, 18   **ii** 45, 63, 72   **iii** 52, 65, 91   **iv** 64, 84, 104

6 Copy the table and then put one number in each space until the table is filled.

5, 6, 10, 15, 24, 25, 27, 40 and 80

Use each number once.

	Factor of 30	Multiple of 8	Odd number
Multiple of 3			
Factor of 40			
Multiple of 5			

How fast can you complete this table? Time yourself.

explanation 3a   explanation 3b

7 **a** Complete this list of the first fifteen prime numbers.

2, 3, 5, 7, …

b What digits do the prime numbers other than 2 and 5 end in?

c Explain your answer to part **b**.

8 Which of the following numbers are prime?

a 53   **b** 78   **c** 87

d 91   **e** 121   **f** 147

g 151   **h** 173   **i** 203

9 Write down three prime numbers which, when their digits are reversed, are also prime. For example, 79 is a prime number and so is 97.

10 Colin has read on the internet that if p is any prime number and n is any integer, the number $n^p - n$ is always divisible by p.

Try this for different values of n and p.

Is this true for all the values you tried?

$$10^3 - 10 = 1000 - 10$$
$$= 990$$

990 is divisible by 3

11 **a** Copy the table and put these numbers in the correct places.

1, 2, 3, 7, 9, 12, 14, 21 and 63

Use each number once and only put one number in each space.

	Factor of 42	Multiple of 3	Prime number
Multiple of 2			
Factor of 27			
Multiple of 7			

b Design a similar table of your own and challenge a friend to complete it.

12 This number machine generates prime numbers for certain integer inputs.

input → | × 4 | → | + 1 | → output

1 → 5   ✓
2 → 9   ✗   NOT PRIME
3 → 13   ✓
4 → 17   ✓
5 → 21   ✗   NOT PRIME
6 → 25   ✗   NOT PRIME

   a Does an input of 7 generate a prime number?

   b List the prime numbers generated by this number machine that are less than 100.

   c Elizabeth notices that these prime numbers can also be expressed as the sum of two square numbers.

   For example, $5 = 2^2 + 1^2$, $13 = 3^2 + 2^2$.

   Is this true for all the prime numbers you have listed?

---

explanation 4 ────────────────────────────────

13 a Copy and complete these factor trees.

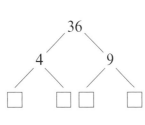

$36 = \square \times \square \times \square \times \square$
$36 = \square^{\square} \times \square^{\square}$

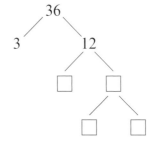

$36 = \square \times \square \times \square \times \square$
$36 = \square^{\square} \times \square^{\square}$

   b What does your answer to part **a** tell you about the factors you use to start the factor tree?

14 Use a factor tree to write each of these numbers as a product of its prime factors.

   a 72   **b** 100   **c** 81   **d** 48

   e 124   **f** 250   **g** 400   **h** 550

explanation 5a   explanation 5b

15 Richard is writing 80 as a product of prime factors.

$$80 = 2 \times 40$$
$$= 2 \times 2 \times 20$$
$$=$$

a Copy and complete his working.

b Use this method to write each of these numbers as a product of prime factors.

i 180   ii 16   iii 495

iv 2600   v 440   vi 900

vii 860   viii 528   ix 14 400   x 1080

16 a The number $2904 = 2^3 \times 3 \times 11^2$.
Explain why 8 is a factor of 2904.

b Write down the first ten factors of 2904 in order of size.

17 a Write 308 as a product of prime factors.

b Use your answer to part **a** to write all of the factors of 308.

18 a Work out 7×13 in your head.

b Write 364 as a product of prime factors.

c Write 3080 as a product of prime factors.

d The teacher simplified the fraction $\frac{350}{616}$ like this:

$$\frac{350}{616} = \frac{2 \times 5^2 \times 7}{2^3 \times 7 \times 11} = \frac{5^2}{2^2 \times 11} = \frac{25}{44}$$

Explain this method.

e Use this method to simplify these fractions.

i $\frac{364}{3080}$ ii $\frac{126}{150}$ iii $\frac{210}{252}$

explanation 6a   explanation 6b

19 a Write each number as the product of prime factors.

$80 = \square \times \square \times \square \times \square \times \square$

$24 = \square \times \square \times \square \times \square$

   b Circle the common factors of 80 and 24.

   c Multiply the common factors together to find the highest common factor (HCF).

20 a Write 60 as a product of prime factors.

   b Write 72 as a product of prime factors.

   c Write the lowest number that contains all the factors in parts **a** and **b**.

   d Write the lowest common multiple of 60 and 72.

21 a Write 12 and 15 as products of prime factors.

   b Find the highest common factor of 12 and 15.

   c Find the lowest common multiple of 12 and 15.

22 Find the prime factors of the numbers in each group and use them to find

    i the highest common factor

    ii the lowest common multiple

a 25, 30	**b** 32, 48	**c** 36, 45
d 55, 66	**e** 84, 96	**f** 130, 165
g 30, 60, 90	**h** 12, 15, 18	**i** 28, 84, 147

Generating sequences

- Generating a sequence from a term–to–term rule
- Using algebra to find missing terms in an arithmetic sequence
- Generating sequences like the Fibonacci sequence

Keywords

You should know

explanation 1

1 Each table shows patterns in a sequence. Copy and complete each table.

a

Pattern					
Position	1	2	3		
Term	3	5			

b

Pattern					
Position	1	2	3		
Term	1	4			

c

Pattern					
Position	1	2	3		
Term	3	7			

explanation 2a   explanation 2b   explanation 2c

2 What is the term-to-term rule for each sequence in question **1**?
State the value of the common differnce, *d*.

3 Write the term-to-term rule for each sequence.

a   2   4   6   8   10

b   1   4   7   10   13

c   3   0   −3   −6   −9

d $\frac{1}{3}$ 0 $-\frac{1}{3}$ $-\frac{2}{3}$

e $\frac{3}{4}$ 1 $\frac{5}{4}$ $\frac{3}{2}$ $\frac{7}{4}$

f   4   1.5   −1   −3.5   −6

4 Write the next two terms in each sequence in question **3**.

5 Copy and complete the table.

	1st term	Term-to-term rule	First five terms
	0	+ 3	0, 3, 6, 9, 12
a	2	+ 5	
b	3	$+ \frac{1}{2}$	
c	−13	+ 3	
d	8	− 5	
e	4	− 1.5	
f	1	− 0.3	
g	−0.5	+ 0.2	
h	−0.5	− 0.4	
i	$\frac{1}{2}$	$+ \frac{1}{3}$	
j	$-\frac{1}{2}$	$+ \frac{1}{5}$	

6 Copy and complete the table.

	1st term	Term-to-term rule	2nd, 3rd, 4th and 5th terms
a	7	+ 5	
b		+ 4	9, 13, 17, 21
c			10, −1, −12, −23
d	−8		−5, −2, 1, 4
e			0.5, −1.5, −3.5, −5.5
f	$\dfrac{1}{2}$	$-\dfrac{1}{2}$	
g			$-\dfrac{1}{4}, -\dfrac{3}{4}, -1\dfrac{1}{4}, -1\dfrac{3}{4}$
h	0.1	+ 0.01	
i			1.10, 1.15, 1.20, 1.25

(explanation 3a)   (explanation 3b)

7 Look at these arithmetic sequences. Some terms in each sequence are missing.

    i What is the common difference, d, for each sequence?

    ii Write the missing terms of each sequence.

a 3, ☐, ☐, 12   **b** 1, ☐, ☐, ☐, 17

c −3, ☐, ☐, ☐, 17   **d** ☐, ☐, 3, ☐, ☐, ☐, 11

e 5, ☐, ☐, ☐, −11   **f** ☐, ☐, 0, ☐, ☐, −12

g ☐, ☐, −8, ☐, ☐, ☐, −28   **h** ☐, ☐, $2\dfrac{1}{2}$, ☐, ☐, 4

i ☐, 3.2, ☐, ☐, ☐, 4   **j** ☐, ☐, 1.3, ☐, ☐, ☐, 0.1

8 Make up three sequences of your own, like those in question **7**.
Pass them to a friend to find the missing terms.
Make sure you have worked out the answers so you can check their answers!

explanation 4

9 These sequences are like the Fibonacci sequence: each term after the second is the sum of the previous two terms.

Work out the missing terms in each sequence.

a   1, 3, 4, ☐, ☐, ☐, ☐

b   2, 4, ☐, ☐, ☐, ☐, ☐

c   3, 6, ☐, ☐, ☐, ☐, ☐

10 Think about sequences like the Fibonacci sequence and the sequences in question **9**.

a   If two consecutive terms in one of these sequences are even, what can you say about the terms in that sequence? Explain how you know.

b   If two consecutive terms in a Fibonacci sequence are odd, what can you say about the terms in that sequence? Explain how you know.

11 a   Hanif adds 1 to each term of the sequence in question **9a**.
Is his new sequence like the Fibonacci sequence? Explain how you know.

b   Jenni multiplies each term of the sequence in question **9a** by 2.
Is her new sequence like the Fibonacci sequence? Explain how you know.

12 Joe wrote a sequence like the Fibonacci sequence.
The fourth term of the sequence was 10.

a   He started with two positive integers. What could they be?

b   How many possible values for the first two terms can you find?

13 Try to find a sequence like the Fibonacci sequence that starts with two positive whole numbers less than 10 and contains the number 100.
How close to 100 can you get? You can use a calculator or a computer to help.

14 Fibonacci was a famous Italian mathematician of the twelfth and thirteen centuries.

Find out what he did and make a mini-poster about him.

Describing sequences

- Generating a sequence from a position–to–term rule
- Describing a sequence using a position–to–term rule
- Writing a position–to–term rule using algebra
- Using the relationship between a term–to–term rule and a rule for the nth term

Keywords

You should know

explanation 1a   explanation 1b

1 Copy and complete the table below for each position-to-term rule.

Position	1	2	3	4	5
Term					

a Position → [+ 2] → Term

b Position → [× 2] → Term

c Position → [× 4] → [− 3] → Term

d Position → [× 1.5] → [− 2] → Term

e Position → [× −2] → [+ 2] → Term

f Position → [− 1] → [× −2] → Term

2 What do you notice about your answers to questions **1e** and **1f**? Why is this?

3 Find the position-to-term rules for these arithmetic sequences.
Write your position-to-term rules as function machines.

a

Position	1	2	3	4	5
Term	6	7	8	9	10

b

Position	1	2	3	4	5
Term	3	6	9	12	15

c

Position	1	2	3	4	5
Term	−4	−8	−12	−16	−20

21

4 Find the position-to-term rules for these arithmetic sequences.

a

Position	1	2	3	4	5
Term	2	5	8	11	14

Write your position-to-term rules as function machines.

Position → $\times d$ → $+ \square$ → Term

b

Position	1	2	3	4	5
Term	3	5	7	9	11

c

Position	1	2	3	4	5
Term	−3	−1	1	3	5

d

Position	1	2	3	4	5
Term	−3	−7	−11	−15	−19

e

Position	1	2	3	4	5
Term	2.5	3	3.5	4	4.5

explanation 2

5 a Convert each position-to-term rule below into an expression for the nth term.

b Calculate the 10th term of each sequence in part **a**.

i Position → $+ 3$ → Term

ii Position → $\times 2$ → $- 3$ → Term

iii Position → $\times 4$ → $- 1$ → Term

iv Position → $\times \frac{1}{2}$ → $+ 3$ → Term

v Position → $\div 2$ → $+ 3$ → Term

6 These are the rules for the nth terms of some arithmetic sequences.
Write the first five terms of each sequence.

a $2n$ **b** $2n - 1$ **c** $3n + 4$ **d** $4n - 4$

e $\frac{1}{2}n + 1$ **f** $-2n$ **g** $-3n + 6$ **h** $-n + 4$

i $-\frac{1}{4}n + 2$ **j** $1 - 3n$ **k** $2(n - 3)$ **l** $\frac{n + 1}{2}$

7 Each table shows an arithmetic sequence.

    i Write the term-to-term rule or difference, d, for each sequence.

    ii Write the rule for the nth term of each sequence.

    iii Write the 100th term of each sequence.

a

Position	1	2	3	4	5
Term	5	9	13	17	21

b

Position	1	2	3	4	5
Term	1	4	7	10	13

c

Position	1	2	3	4	5
Term	7	9	11	13	15

d

Position	1	2	3	4	5
Term	−3	−1	1	3	5

e

Position	1	2	3	4	5
Term	−2	−4	−6	−8	−10

f

Position	1	2	3	4	5
Term	$-\frac{1}{2}$	0	$\frac{1}{2}$	1	$1\frac{1}{2}$

g

Position	1	2	3	4	5
Term	$3\frac{1}{2}$	4	$4\frac{1}{2}$	5	$5\frac{1}{2}$

8 What do you notice about the common differences, d, and the rules for the nth terms for the arithmetic sequences in question 7?

9 Copy and complete these sentences.

    a The expression for the nth term is $3n + 1$. The term-to-term rule is …

    b The expression for the nth term is $-3n + 1$. The term-to-term rule is …

    e The expression for the nth term is $-5n - 2$. The term-to-term rule is …

    d The difference is $+ 2$. A possible expression for the nth term is …

    e The difference is $- 7$. A possible expression for the nth term is …

    f The difference is $-\frac{1}{4}$. A possible expression for the nth term is …

10 Write an expression for the nth term of these arithmetic sequences.

    a 4, 5, 6, 7, 8   **b** −2, 1, 4, 7, 10   **c** 12, 22, 32, 42, 52

    d −3, 2, 7, 12, 17   **e** 7, 13, 19, 25, 31   **f** 0, −1, −2, −3, −4

    g 6, 4, 2, 0, −2   **h** 23, 18, 13, 8, 3   **i** −5.5, −5, −4.5, −4, −3.5

11 Angus has spilt ink over his homework.

    The ink covers parts of four arithmetic sequences.

    Make a copy for him, completing all the boxes correctly.

Position	1	2	3	4	5	6	n
a	▉	5	7	9	▉	13	▉
b	14	▉	▉	5	▉	−1	▉
c	▉	−2	▉	▉	▉	0	$\frac{n}{2} - 3$
d	5.7	▉	▉	▉	6.5	▉	▉

12 The oval contains sequences. The rectangle contains expressions for nth terms. Four of the sequences match four of the expressions.

    a Which sequence matches which nth term?

    b Write the first five terms of the sequence that matches the remaining nth term.

    c Write a possible expression for the nth term of the remaining sequence.

    d Which of the nth terms give sequences that are *not* arithmetic?

    i ..., 71, 78, 85, 92, 99, ...

    ii ..., $3\frac{1}{2}$, $5\frac{1}{2}$, $7\frac{1}{2}$, $9\frac{1}{2}$, ...

    iii ..., 34.5, 34.8, 35.1, 35.4, ...

    iv ..., −68, −75, −82, −89, ...

    v ..., $\frac{1}{23}$, $\frac{1}{27}$, $\frac{1}{31}$, $\frac{1}{35}$, ...

    A $\dfrac{3n}{10} + 30$

    B $\dfrac{1}{4n + 3}$

    C $2 - 7n$

    D $7n - 13$

    E $\dfrac{2}{n + 3}$

13 Jules is making staircase patterns using square tiles.

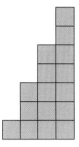

The first step is 1 tile high.
After that, each step is 2 tiles higher than the one before.
The second step is 3 tiles high, the third is 5 tiles high,
and so on. The diagram shows the pattern with 4 steps.

a **i** Jules continues the pattern, and writes down the heights
  of the first six steps. Copy and complete his list.
  1, 3, 5, ☐, ☐, ☐

  ii Write an expression for the height of the *n*th step.

  iii Write down the height of the 20th step.

b Jules makes two copies of his 4-step pattern and fits them
  together to form a rectangle, as shown.

  i How many tiles are there in the rectangle?

  ii Use your answer to write down the value of 1 + 3 + 5 + 7.
  Explain how you know.

c Jules makes two identical 20-step patterns.
  He fits them together to make a rectangle as described in part **b**.

  i What is the width of the rectangle? What is its length?

  ii Use your answers to work out the sum of the first 20 odd numbers.

  iii Describe an easy way to add the first 20 terms of any arithmetic sequence.

14 The school theatre has rows with different numbers of seats.
Row A has 13 seats, row B has 15 seats, row C has 17 seats and so on.
All the rows are lettered in alphabetical order up to and including T.

a How many seats are there in row H?

b How many seats in row Q?

c How many seats are there in total in the theatre?

15 One of the machines in a screw factory has developed a fault.

Each screw *should* be 25.4 mm long. In fact, the first screw was 25.39 mm long,
the second was 25.38 mm, the third was 25.37 mm and so on.

a What was the length of the 50th screw?

b The machine was stopped after a screw of length 16.07 mm was produced.
How many incorrect screws were made?

Angles

- Identifying alternate and corresponding angles
- Proving that the angles of any triangle add up to 180° and that the angles of any quadrilateral add up to 360°
- Knowing that the exterior angle of a triangle is equal to the sum of the two interior opposite angles
- Solving problems using properties of angles formed by parallel and intersecting lines
- Calculating the sum of the interior angles of quadrilaterals, pentagons and hexagons
- Calculating the interior and exterior angles of a regular polygon

Keywords

You should know

explanation 1a   explanation 1b   explanation 1c

1 Calculate the size of each angle marked by a letter.
Give reasons for your answers.

a

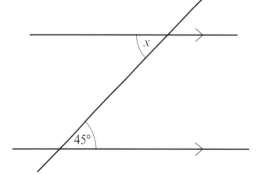

b

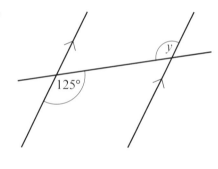

c

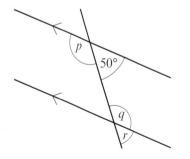

d

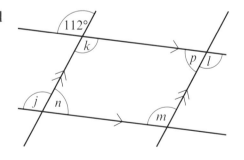

explanation 2a   explanation 2b   explanation 2c   explanation 2d

2 Calculate the size of each angle marked by a letter.
Give reasons for your answers.

a

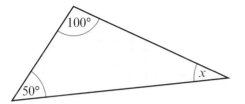

b

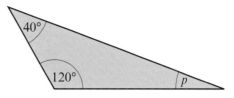

c

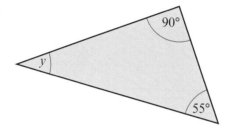

d

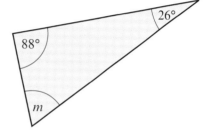

3 Calculate the size of each angle marked by a letter.
Give reasons for your answers.

a

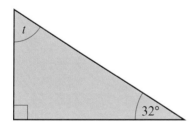

b

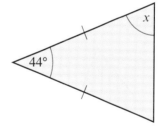

4 Calculate the size of each angle marked by a letter.
Give reasons for your answers.

a

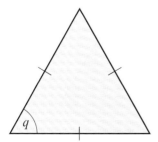

b

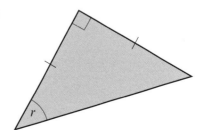

5 Calculate the size of each angle marked by a letter.
Give reasons for your answers.

a

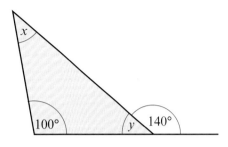

b

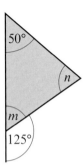

c

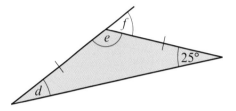

d

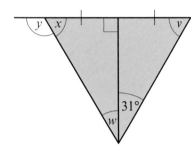

---

explanation 3

6 Calculate the size of each angle marked by a letter.
Give reasons for your answers.

a

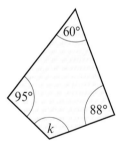

b

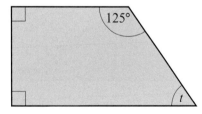

c

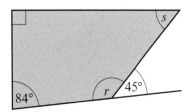

d

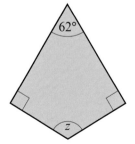

7 Calculate the size of each angle marked by a letter.
Give reasons for your answers.

a

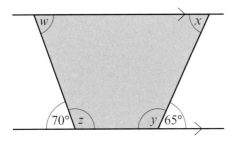

b

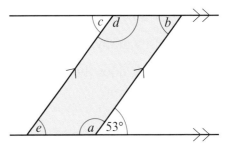

c

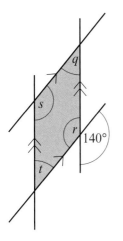

d

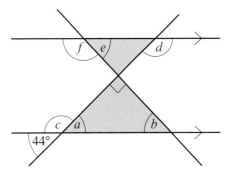

e

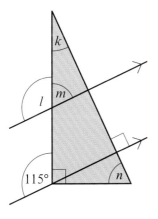

f

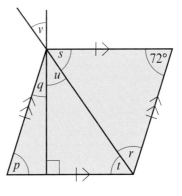

g

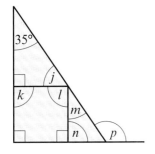

h

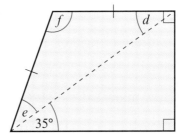

explanation 4a | explanation 4b

8 Draw a pentagon. From one vertex, draw all the possible diagonals.

   a How many triangles have you made?

   b What does this tell you about the sum of the interior angles of any pentagon?

9 Repeat question **8** for a hexagon.

10 A polygon is regular if all its interior angles (and its sides) are the same size. Copy and complete the table. Use what you discovered in questions **8** and **9**.

Regular polygon	Number of sides	Sum of interior angles	Size of each interior angle	Size of each exterior angle	Sum of exterior angles
Equilateral triangle	3	$1 \times 180°$ $= 180°$	$180° \div 3$ $= 60°$	$180° - 60°$ $= 120°$	$120° \times 3$ $= 360°$
Square	4				
Pentagon	5				
Hexagon	6				
Heptagon	7				
Octagon	8				
Nonagon	9				
Decagon	10				
Dodecagon	12				

11 Write a general statement about the interior and exterior angles of any regular polygon. Use your answers to question **10** to help you.

12 Each interior angle of a regular polygon is 178°.

   a What is the size of each exterior angle?

   b How many sides does the regular polygon have?

13 The Citadelle of Lille, France, was built by Vauban between 1667 and 1670. The diagram shows a plan of it. It is based on a regular pentagon, has 5 lines of symmetry, and has rotation symmetry of order 5.

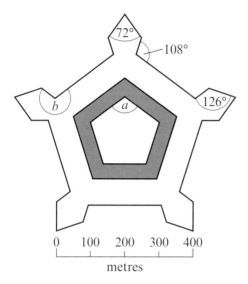

a   How many sides does the outside wall have?

b   Calculate the size of angles a and b.

c   What is the sum of all the interior angles of the outside wall?

14 Bhavna has some tiles shaped like regular pentagons. Each one has two red edges. She fits them together so that the red edges meet, as shown.

a   i   Calculate the angle x.

ii   She continues the pattern by adding more tiles. Will the pattern join up with the first tile again, without overlapping? Explain how you decided. You may find your table from question **10** useful.

iii   If the pattern does join up, how many tiles will it contain?

b   Repeat part **a** using regular hexagons instead of pentagons.

c   Repeat part **a** using regular heptagons.

d   Repeat part **a** using regular octagons.

Lines, shapes and coordinates

- Classifying quadrilaterals by their geometric properties
- Calculating the midpoint of a line segment
- Knowing the parts of a circle

Keywords

You should know

explanation 1

1 Look at this flow chart. It shows a possible way to classify quadrilaterals.

a Which catergory contains arrowheads?

b Name the two shapes that belong to **A**.

c Do either of the shapes in **A** have just one pair of parallel sides?

d Are there any shapes in **B** that have all sides the same length?

e Are there any rectangles in **A**? Explain your answer.

f Are there any rectangles in **C**? Explain your answer.

g Are there any squares in **B**? Explain your answer.

h Name the two shapes that belong to **B**.

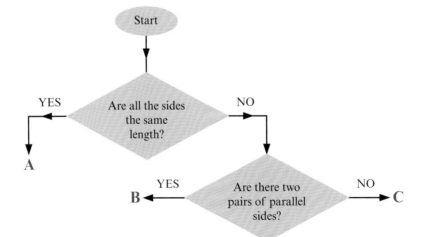

2 Which quadrilaterals always have each property?

a All sides are the same length.

b All angles are the same size.

c Opposite sides are equal.

d Opposite angles are equal.

e There are two pairs of parallel sides.

f There is only one pair of parallel sides.

g Diagonals are of the same length.

h The diagonals intersect at right angles.

i There is only one line of reflection symmetry.

j There are two lines of reflection symmetry.

k There are four lines of reflection symmetry.

l It has rotational symmetry of order 2.

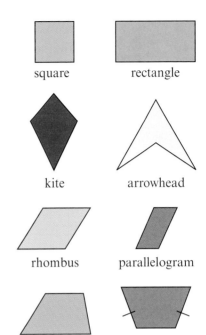

3 Look at this flow chart. It shows a possible way to classify the quadrilaterals according to their symmetry properties.

Write a shape that could be in each tray. Use your answers to question **2**, and other properties of quadrilaterals, to help you.

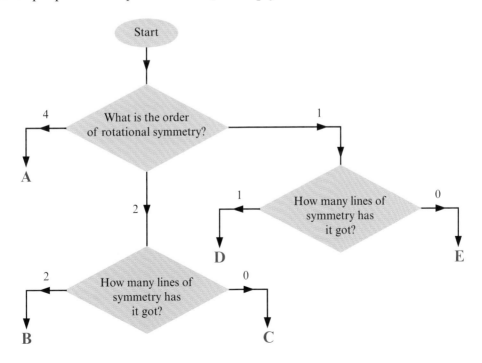

4 In each grid, three vertices of a quadrilateral are plotted.
Write down all the possible coordinates of the fourth vertex.

a A rectangle

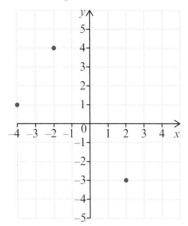

b A rhombus

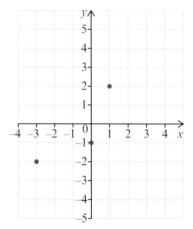

c A kite

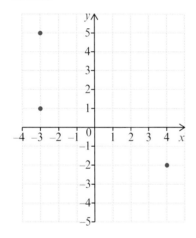

d An arrowhead

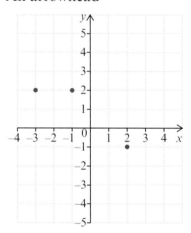

e A parallelogram

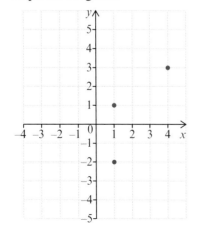

f An isosceles trapezium that contains the origin (0, 0)

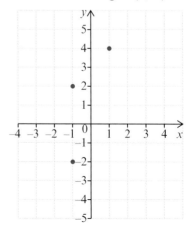

5 The diagram shows two vertices of a square. Find all the possible positions of the other two vertices. Write their coordinates.

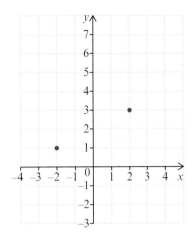

explanation 2a   explanation 2b   explanation 2c

6 Write the coordinates of the midpoint of each line segment.

a

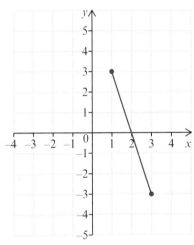

b

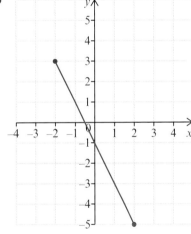

c

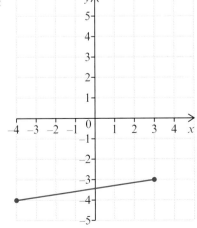

d

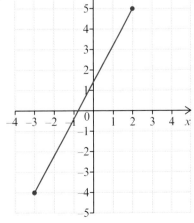

7 These are the coordinates of the end points of line segments.
Calculate the coordinates of the midpoint of each line segment.

  a (2, 4) and (4, 8) **b** (0, 2) and (6, 2) **c** (2, –3) and (–1, 6)

8 Point M is the midpoint of line segment AB. The coordinates of points A and M are given. In each case, calculate the coordinates of point B.

  a A(1, 2), M(5, 3) **b** A(–2, 1), M(4, –1) **c** A(3, –8), M(1, –4)

explanation 3a   explanation 3b

9 Draw a circle with radius 5 cm.
Mark two points P and Q on the circumference so that PQ = 10 cm.

  a What is line PQ called?

  b Mark another point R on the circumference of the circle.
Draw the lines PR and QR. Measure the angle PRQ.

  c Repeat part **b** for some other positions of point R on the circumference.
What do you notice about the angle PRQ each time?

10 Draw a circle with radius 5 cm. Mark a point A on the circumference.
Mark another point B on the circumference so that AB = 5 cm.

  a What is the line AB called?

  b Mark a point C on the major arc of the circle and draw lines AC and BC.
Measure angle ACB. Is it acute or obtuse?

  c Repeat part **b** for some other positions of the point C on the major arc.
What do you notice about the size of angle ACB?

  d Mark a point D on the minor arc of the circle and draw lines AD and BD.
Measure the angle ADB. Is it acute or obtuse?

  e Repeat part **d** for some other positions of point D on the minor arc.
What do you notice about the size of angle ADB?

  f What do you notice about the sum of angles ACB and ADB?
Does it depend on where points C and D are?

  g Jacqui draws a quadrilateral by joining up any four points on the
circumference of a circle.
What do you expect the sum of opposite angles to be?
Explain your answer. Check your answer by drawing and measuring.

Constructions (1)

- Constructing a perpendicular bisector
- Bisecting an angle
- Constructing a perpendicular from a point to a line
- Constructing a perpendicular from a point on a line
- Using a ruler and compasses to construct a right–angled triangle, given the longest side and another side

Keywords

You should know

explanation 1a   explanation 1b   explanation 1c   explanation 1d

1 Practise using a pair of compasses to construct perpendicular bisectors of lines that are not horizontal or vertical.

Make sure that you are confident that you can do this type of construction well.

2 Using a ruler and pencil, draw triangle ABC on squared paper.

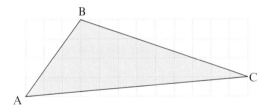

a Construct the perpendicular bisector of side AB.

b Construct the perpendicular bisector of side BC.

c What do you notice about the distance of the point of intersection of the two perpendicular bisectors from A, B and C?

3 The diagram shows a shoreline.

Three people stand at A, B and C. They each see a boat out at sea. The boat is equidistant from each of the three people.

Copy the diagram. By construction, locate the position of the boat, P.

Use what you found out in question **2** to help you.

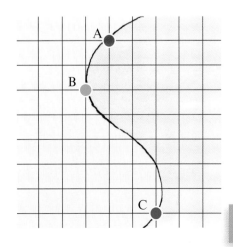

explanation 2a explanation 2b explanation 2c explanation 2d

4 Practise using a pair of compasses to construct angle bisectors.
Bisect angles of different sizes, including some acute and some obtuse.
Make sure that you are confident that you can do this type of construction well.

5 a Using a protractor, draw an angle of 70°.

  b By construction, bisect the angle.

  c Using a protractor, check that the angle has been bisected.

6 Draw triangle XYZ on squared paper.

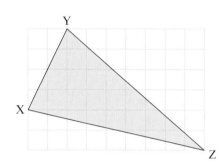

  a By construction, bisect angle X.

  b By construction, bisect angles Y and Z.

  c What do you notice about the three angle bisectors?

7 The diagram shows a field PQRS.

The farmer wants to plant a hedge that bisects the corner of his field at P.

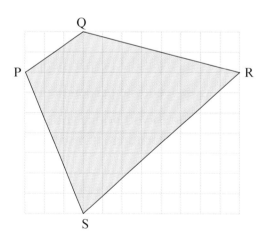

  a Copy the diagram onto squared paper.

  b By construction, show where the hedge will be planted.

8 You can construct an angle by bisecting a larger one.

  a Draw a line and construct the perpendicular bisector.

  b By construction, show how an angle of 45° can be formed.

explanation 3a   explanation 3b   explanation 3c   explanation 3d

9 Practise using a pair of compasses to construct the perpendicular from a
point to a line that is not horizontal or vertical.
Make sure that you are confident that you can do this type of construction well.

10 Copy this diagram onto squared paper.

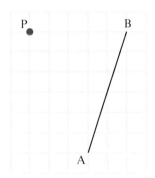

   a Construct the shortest line segment
from P to the line AB.

      Label the point where the two lines meet Q.

   b You can construct an angle of 45° by bisecting
a right angle.

      Without using a protractor, mark and label
a point R so that angle PQR = 45° and PQ = QR.

11 Copy triangle ABC onto centimetre-squared paper.

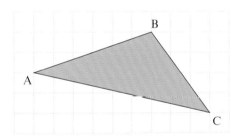

   a Construct the line perpendicular to BC that passes through A.
You may find it helpful to extend line BC.

      Mark the point X on this line so that B lies on XC.

   b The area of triangle ABC is given by

$$\frac{1}{2} \times \text{length BC} \times \text{length AX}$$

      By measuring BC and AX, calculate the area of the triangle.

explanation 4a   explanation 4b   explanation 4c

12 Practise constructing a perpendicular from a point on a line that is not
horizontal or vertical. Make sure that you are confident that you can do this
type of construction well.

13 Using a ruler and protractor, copy the parallelogram WXYZ.

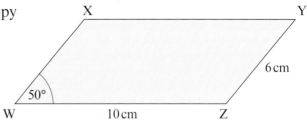

a By construction, bisect angle WZY.

b Mark a point, P, 4 cm from Z on the line constructed in part **a**.

c Construct the shortest line from P to the line WZ. Measure its length.

d Construct the shortest line from P to YZ. Measure its length.

14 Follow the instructions to draw a diagram. Make a sketch first.

a Draw a line PQ 8 cm long. Mark two points X and Y on it so that PX = 3 cm and PY = 5 cm.

b Construct perpendiculars to the line PQ, passing through X and Y. Label the lines XW and YZ.

c Mark a point S on XW so that XS = 4 cm.

d Mark a point R on YZ so that YR = 4 cm.

e Draw the quadrilateral PQRS. What type of quadrilateral is PQRS?

f Measure the lengths PS and QR.

(explanation 5)

15 Draw a right-angled triangle where the longest side is 13 cm and another side is 5 cm.
Measure the length of the third side.

16 A painter rests her ladder against a wall. The ladder is 8 metres long and rests on the horizontal ground 2 metres from the wall.

a Use 1 cm to represent 1 m to construct a scale diagram.

b Measure how far up the wall the ladder rests, and the angle it makes with the ground.

17 Construct a quadrilateral ABCD with a diagonal AC of 10 cm, two opposite sides of 6 cm and 7 cm, and two right angles that are not cut by AC.

Chance and probability

- Calculating the probability of an event for equally likely outcomes
- Constructing a sample space diagram
- Understanding that random processes are unpredictable

Keywords

You should know

explanation 1a   explanation 1b   explanation 1c

1 Lee has four groups of beads. He chooses two groups, mixes them up in a tin and a bead is selected at random.

group 1   group 2   group 3   group 4

a The probability of choosing a red is 1.
Which two groups did he mix in the tin and what is the probability of picking a yellow bead?

b Which two groups should he mix to get the lowest probability of picking a red?

c Which two groups should he mix to get an even chance of picking a red or yellow bead?

2 a Lee mixes all the groups from question **1** in the tin.
What is the probability of picking these beads?

  i a red bead   **ii** a yellow bead

b Lee adds one more red bead and one more yellow bead to the tin.
What effect does this have on the probability of choosing each colour bead?
Explain your answer.

explanation 2a   explanation 2b   explanation 2c

3 An experiment consists of rolling a dice.

    a Draw a sample space diagram.

    b Describe an event where the outcome is impossible.

    c Draw a sample space diagram with an event that has
       an even chance of happening.

    d Describe an event that is certain to happen.

    e The dice is rolled 100 times.
       How many times would you expect to get a prime number?

    f Sam rolled the dice 30 times and got a prime number 17 times.
       Is there anything wrong?

4 A pack of 52 playing cards is shuffled and the top card is turned over.

    a Describe the sample space.

    b Describe these events.

       i An impossible event

      ii A certain event

     iii An event with an even chance

    c What is the probability of turning over a heart?

    d John shuffles the cards, looks at the top card then puts it back.
       He repeats this 12 times. How many hearts would he expect to see?

    e Repeat John's experiment. How many hearts did you get?
       Explain any differences.

5 Nadeem, David, Cathy and Kim each have six counters. The counters are either
red, blue or yellow and they each select a counter at random.

    a Nadeem has two yellow counters. What other counters must Nadeem have if
       the probability of choosing a red counter is 0?

    b The probability that David chooses a blue counter is $\frac{1}{2}$.

       Describe the possibilities for the colour of David's counters.

    c What colour counters does Cathy have if the probability of choosing red is $\frac{1}{3}$
       and the probability of choosing yellow is $\frac{1}{2}$?

6 Zak has a set of ten different cards. He chooses a card at random.

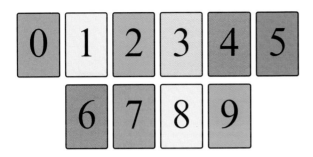

a How many possible outcomes are there?

b What is the probability that he chooses an odd number?

c What is the probability that he chooses a prime number?

d What is the probability that he chooses a multiple of 8?

e What is the probability that he chooses a factor of 36?

7 David, Kim and Zoe design a poster.
They want to add their names to the bottom.
To decide the order they write each name on a piece
of paper, put it in a box and get a friend to pull the
names out at random.

1st	2nd	3rd
D	K	Z
D		

a Complete the list to show the sample space.

b What is the probability that a girl's name is first?

c David does not think this method is fair because there is more chance that a
girl will be first. Is he right?

8 Sarah is carrying out an experiment with a coin.

a If her coin is fair, how many heads should she expect to get in 12 throws?

b Sarah throws the coin 12 times and gets 9 heads.

  i Do you think that her coin must be biased?

  ii What could she do to make her experiment more reliable?

9 Three different scratch cards, A, B and C, all have some coloured squares as shown below. All 12 squares on each card are hidden, and you may reveal just one square on each card.

A    B 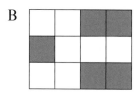   C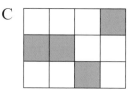

a On which card are you most likely to reveal a hidden coloured square?

b Explain your answer to part **a**.

c Here are two more scratch cards.

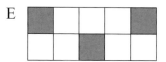

Peter thinks there is less chance of revealing a coloured square on card E than on card D because they are more spaced out. Is he right?

10 Two bags contain red, blue and green counters.
Copy and complete each table.

a

Event	Number	Probability of event
Pick red	5	
Pick green	3	
Pick blue		$\frac{1}{5}$

b

Event	Number	Probability of event
Pick red	6	
Pick green		$\frac{1}{3}$
Pick blue	10	

Probability

- Finding the probability of an event not occurring
- Using diagrams to record all possible outcomes for two events
- Using diagrams to record all possible outcomes for two successive events

Keywords

You should know

explanation 1a   explanation 1b

1 A bag contains two 2p coins, three 10p coins and four £1 coins.
   A coin is taken out of the bag at random.

   a Find these probabilities as fractions.

      i P(2p coin)   ii P(£1 coin)

     iii P(10p coin)   iv P(not a £1 coin)

   b Find P(2p coin) + P(10p coin) + P(£1 coin). Explain your answer.

2 A game uses a ten-sided spinner, numbered from 1 to 10.
   Give, as decimals, the probabilities of these events.

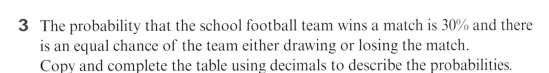

   a seven   b an even number

   c a multiple of three   d a factor of twelve

   e a prime number   f a square number

3 The probability that the school football team wins a match is 30% and there
   is an equal chance of the team either drawing or losing the match.
   Copy and complete the table using decimals to describe the probabilities.

Event	Win	Draw	Lose
Probability			

4 There are four blue, eight red and some yellow beads in a jar.
One bead is taken from the jar at random. The probability

that it is yellow is $\frac{1}{3}$.

   a Explain why the total number of beads in the jar
must be a multiple of 3.

   b Find   **i** P(red)   **ii** P(blue)

5 In a class of 32 pupils, 16 play football (F), 11 play badminton (B) and 8 play
tennis (T). Only 3 students play all three sports but 5 play both football and
badminton, 4 play both badminton and tennis and 4 play both football and tennis.

   a Simon draws a diagram to represent this information.

      Explain why he has put 3 where the three circles overlap.

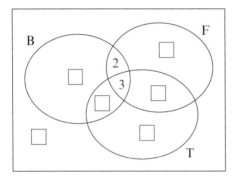

   b Next he puts 2 in the area for F and B only. Is he right?

   c Copy and complete the diagram.

   d One person is chosen at random.
Find the probability that they play these sports.

      i football only   **ii** none of these sports   **iii** exactly two of the sports

6 A school sells 300 raffle tickets. Tina has bought 4 tickets.
She did not win first prize or second prize.
What is the probability that she wins the third prize?

explanation 2a   explanation 2b

7 Copy and complete the table.

Event	Probability that event occurs	Probability that it does not occur
Getting a double six with two dice	$\frac{1}{36}$	
Snow in January	0.58	
Choosing a king from a pack of cards		
Manchester City win a home match	72%	

8 a The box contains a set of pool balls. One ball is chosen at random. Find these probabilities.

   i P(striped)   **ii** P(not striped)

  iii P(black 8)   **iv** P(not black 8)

   v P(prime number)   **vi** P(striped or even numbered)

b The white ball is removed and Gary then chooses one ball at random. It is number 12.

He keeps this ball and selects a second ball at random. Find these probabilities.

   i P(second ball is higher than 12)   **ii** P(second ball is a factor of 12)

9 Sally spins the wheel of colour and it lands on blue. Work out the probability that her second spin lands on these colours.

  a red   **b** blue

  c pink   **d** blue or pink

  e not blue   **f** not blue or pink

10 Linda's dad picks her up every Tuesday after dance class.
The probability that he is early is 0.95 and that he arrives on time is 0.03.
What is the probability that he is late?

11 Kevin has a bag containing the old coins shown.

These are the probabilities of picking particular coins.

half penny   penny

threepence sixpence   shilling

P(halfpenny) = 0.15   P(penny) = 0.3

P(threepence) = 0.2   P(sixpence) = 0.12

What are these probabilities?

a P(copper or brass coin)   **b** P(threepence or a sixpence)

c P(not a threepence)   **d** P(shilling)

12 The probability that Lucy hands her homework in on time is 0.75.
The probability that she hands it in early is 0.1.
What is the probability that she hands her homework in late?

13 One tile is chosen at random from the rack.

Find these probabilities.

C_3 Z_{10} E_1 B_3 E_1 O_1 F_4

a P(vowel)

b P(not a vowel)

c P(the value of the tile is a factor of 30)

explanation 3a   explanation 3b

14 Colin is making a list of all outcomes when three coins are flipped.

1st coin	2nd coin	3rd coin
H	H	H
H	H	T
H	T	H
H	T	T
T		

a Colin has started to show the sample space in this table. Explain how Colin is making his table.

b Copy and complete the sample space.

c Find the probability of getting three heads.

d Find the probability of getting exactly one head.

e Find the probability of getting more heads than tails.

15 A fruit machine has two cylinders with three types of fruit on each. The cylinders are spun round and each fruit is equally likely to appear. The illustration shows the outcome of cherries and a banana.

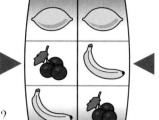

   a List all the possible outcomes.

   b What is the probability of getting two identical fruit?

   c What is the probability of getting at least one lemon?

   d What is the probability of getting no lemons?

16 A college has four 5-a-side football teams A, B, C, and D. Teams A and D are all-girl teams. Each team plays every other team once. The referee writes down all the possible pairs on paper and puts them in a bag then selects the first pair at random.

   a Write what was on the six pieces of paper in the bag.

   b What is the probability that teams A and D play the first match?

17 Two four-sided barrels are each labelled with the digits 0, 1, 2 and 3.

Each barrel is spun to make a two-digit number. 03 is 3, 00 is zero.

	second digit			
first digit	0	1	2	3
0	00	01		
1	10			
2				
3				

   a Copy and complete the sample space diagram.

   b What is the probability of getting a prime number?

   c What is the probability of getting a multiple of 8?

   d What is the probability of getting a factor of 30?

   e What is the probability of getting a multiple of 9?

18 a Abida rolls a red and a blue dice, each numbered from 1 to 6. She adds the scores together. Copy and complete the sample space diagram to show all the possible outcomes.

b Which outcome is most likely?

c Use the diagram to find these probabilities.

   i P(the same number on both dice)

   ii P(the sum of the numbers is less than 10)

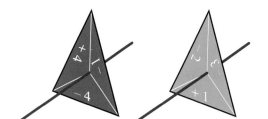

2					
				7	
		6			
					10
			9		
8					

   iii P(the score on the red dice is exactly double the score on the blue dice)

19 Piers spins two three-sided spinners. He adds the two results. The total score shown is −4 + +1 = −4 + 1 = −3.

a Copy and complete the sample space diagram.

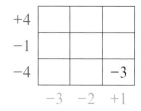

+4			
−1			
−4			−3
	−3	−2	+1

b What is the probability of each event?

   i The total score is negative.

   ii The total score is positive.

   iii The total score is zero.

   iv The total score is 4.

   v The total score is greater than −4.

20 Tony spins two five-sided spinners, both with sides numbered 1, 2, 3, 4 and 5. He multiplies together the two numbers landed on. Draw a sample space diagram to show all the possible outcomes. Use your diagram to find these probabilities.

a P(an even number)

b P(an odd number)

c P(a multiple of 3)

d P(a factor of 24)

e P(a factor of 3600)

Experimental probability

- Using experimental data to estimate probabilities
- Understanding the effect of repeating an experiment many times
- Comparing theoretical and experimental probabilities

Keywords

You should know

explanation 1a   explanation 1b   explanation 1c

1 John cut an isosceles triangle from thin card.
He found the centre by joining each corner to
the midpoint of the opposite side.

He pushed a short stick through the centre to form a spinner.

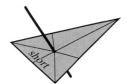

a John spins the spinner 20 times to see what happens.
He records whether it lands on the short side or on one of the longer sides.
What is the likelihood of the spinner landing on the short side?

Short	Long

b John decides to estimate the
probability that the spinner lands
on the short side.
He spins it forty times.
Find the relative frequency of it landing on the short side as a decimal.

Event	Short	Long
Frequency	8	32

c To check his results John spins the spinner 55 times and then spins it 120 times.

Event	Short	Long
Frequency	11	44

Event	Short	Long
Frequency	28	92

Find the relative frequency of landing on the short side for each set of data
to 3 decimal places.

d Use the set of data you think will be most reliable to find the best estimate
for the probability of the spinner coming to rest on the shortest side.

2 Design your own spinner and investigate the probability that it lands on a
particular side.

3 Simon flipped a coin 5 times and got 3 heads.
He then flipped it another 5 times and got another 3 heads.
After another 5 goes he got 2 more heads.
He recorded his data in a table.

Number of trials	5	10	15	20	25	30
Number of heads	3	6	8			
Relative frequency	$\frac{3}{5} = 0.6$	$\frac{6}{10} = 0.6$	$\frac{8}{15} = 0.533$			

a Use a coin to complete a table like Simon's.

b Comment on the relative frequency of getting a head.

c What is your experimental probability of getting a head?

4 The lifetimes of 500 light bulbs are given in the table.

Lifetime	Frequency
0–99 hours	150
100–199 hours	300
200–299 hours	50

Estimate the probability that a similar bulb will last at least 200 hours.

5 A teacher puts 20 discs in a bag, some are red and some are blue. He writes three possible numbers for the red and blue discs on the board. One pupil takes a disc at random from the bag and the result is recorded. The disc is replaced and the next pupil picks a disc.

How many red and blue discs are in the bag?

Possibilities
A 7 red and 13 blue
B 5 red and 15 blue
C 3 red and 17 blue

a Write down the theoretical probabilities, as decimals, of getting a red disc and getting a blue disc for each of the possible combinations A, B and C

Results:
B B B R B B B B
R B B B B B R B
B R B B B B B B
B B R B B R B B

b Find the relative frequency of getting each colour based on the data collected in the class and compare them to theoretical probabilities.

c How many red and blue discs do you think the teacher had in the bag? How certain are you?

6 Choose possibility A, B or C from question **5**. Put the correct number of red and blue cubes in a box. Ask a partner to select a random cube from the box and record the result before replacing it. Repeat this forty times and then compare the relative frequencies with the theoretical probabilities.

Could your partner predict how many blue and red cubes there were?

7 The table shows the results in the Premiership at one stage in the football season.

Home wins	24
Away wins	9
Draws	5

   a Use these results to estimate the probability of these outcomes in a randomly chosen match the next week. Give your answers as fractions.

      i home win   **ii** away win   **iii** draw.

These were the results much later in the season.

Home wins	182
Away wins	100
Draws	98

   b What is the probability of each outcome in part **a** based on this table?

   c Will your answers to part **a** or part **b** be more reliable? Why?

8 In a set of thirty cards some are marked with a cross and the others left blank. The number of cards marked with a cross is a multiple of 4. The cards are shuffled then a card is chosen at random. Its marking is recorded, 'X' for a cross and 'B' for blank. Then it is returned and the cards are shuffled again. These are the results.

   XBXBXXXBXBBBXBBXXBBXXXBB

   a How many trials were carried out?

   b Summarise the data in a table.

   c Find the relative frequency of getting a cross.

   d What is the experimental probability of getting a cross?

   e Compare the experimental probability with the possible theoretical probabilities.

   f How many cards out of thirty does this suggest were marked with a cross?

9 Make a set of ten blank cards and mark either 3, 6 or 9 cards with a cross. See if your partner can use experimental probability to find out how many are marked with a cross.

10 Every week for one year Kevin's grandma put either a 50p or a £2 coin into his moneybox, which has only one opening at the top for money.
He shakes the moneybox and then turns it upside down and shakes again until a coin falls out.
He records which coin fell out then puts the coin back in.
He does this 20 times with these results.

50p, £2, £2, 50p, £2, 50p, £2, 50p, £2, 50p, £2, £2, 50p, £2, £2, £2, 50p, £2, 50p, £2

a Summarise his results in a table.

b Calculate the relative frequency of each coin.

c Estimate the probability of getting each coin.

d Explain how Kevin could estimate how much money he has in his moneybox.

11 Use a paper clip and a pencil to make this spinner. Spin the paper clip round the pencil point and record where the middle of the clip lands.

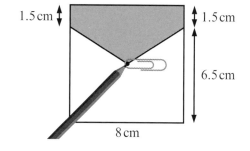

a Decide how many times to spin the paper clip. Do the experiment and record your results in a table.

b Use your results to estimate the probability of the paper clip landing in the shaded region.

c Measure the angle at the centre of the shaded region and calculate the theoretical probability of the clip landing in this region.

d Compare the theoretical and experimental probabilities.

e How could you improve the reliability of the experimental probability?

Fractions and decimals

- Using division to convert fractions to decimals
- Understanding that a recurring decimal is a fraction
- Ordering fractions

Keywords

You should know

explanation 1

1 Write each decimal as a fraction in its lowest terms.

a   0.8
b   0.45
c   0.72
d   0.98

e   0.125
f   0.255
g   0.312
h   0.782

2 Change these decimals to mixed numbers and simplify as far as possible.

a   2.75
b   14.35
c   55.55
d   36.625

e   79.235
f   124.452
g   163.128
h   201.402

explanation 2a   explanation 2b   explanation 2c

3 Use division to change these fractions to decimals.

a $\dfrac{1}{5}$
b $\dfrac{3}{8}$
c $\dfrac{9}{5}$
d $\dfrac{23}{4}$
e $\dfrac{37}{8}$

For the questions that follow, you can use a calculator.

4 Use a calculator to write each fraction as a decimal.

a $\dfrac{1}{40}$
b $\dfrac{1}{16}$
c $\dfrac{2}{22}$
d $\dfrac{5}{33}$

e $\dfrac{3}{50}$
f $\dfrac{45}{32}$
g $\dfrac{126}{75}$
h $\dfrac{99}{45}$

55

5 This table shows the amount of homework Amy had last week.

Subject	Maths	English	Science	History	Geography	RS	French	Art	Music
Minutes	50	45	55	30	30	15	35	20	20

    a What was the total time Amy spent on homework last week?

    b What fraction of that time did she spend on each subject?

    c Change each of the fractions in part **b** into a decimal.

6 a Use a calculator to help you write $\frac{1}{3}$ as a decimal.

    b What do you notice about the answer on the calculator display?

    c Write down what you think $\frac{2}{3}$ will be as a decimal.

    d Check your answer using a calculator.

    e Write down what you think $\frac{3}{3}$ will be as a decimal.

    f Use your answers to explain why 0.999… = 1.

    g Predict the decimal forms of $\frac{4}{3}, \frac{5}{3}, \frac{6}{3}$ and $\frac{7}{3}$.

7 Using $\frac{1}{3} = 0.333…$ work out the decimal equivalents of $\frac{1}{6}, \frac{1}{9}$, and $\frac{1}{12}$.

8 a Work out $\frac{1}{9} + \frac{1}{11}$ writing your answer as a fraction.

    b Find $\frac{1}{9}$ and $\frac{1}{11}$ as decimals and add them together.

    c What do you notice about your answers to parts **a** and **b**?

    d Use your results to predict $\frac{17}{99}$ as a decimal.

    e Now predict $\frac{1}{99}$ as a decimal.

    f What do you think $\frac{1}{999}, \frac{547}{999}$ and $\frac{58}{999}$ will be as decimals?

9 a Convert each fraction to a decimal.

    i $\frac{1}{2}$ **ii** $\frac{2}{3}$ **iii** $\frac{3}{7}$ **iv** $\frac{7}{9}$

    v $\frac{5}{11}$ **vi** $\frac{6}{15}$ **vii** $\frac{7}{16}$ **viii** $\frac{11}{12}$

    b **i** Which fractions in part **a** give terminating decimals?

       ii Which fractions in part **a** give recurring decimals?

10 Write three recurring decimals and their equivalent fractions.

11 Copy and complete this table of sevenths.

Fraction	$\frac{1}{7}$	$\frac{2}{7}$	$\frac{3}{7}$	$\frac{4}{7}$	$\frac{5}{7}$	$\frac{6}{7}$
Decimal	$0.142\,857\,14\ldots$					

What do you notice about the decimals?

explanation 3a   explanation 3b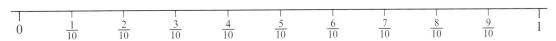

12 Write the fractions in each group in order of size, smallest first.

   a $\frac{1}{4}, \frac{1}{5}, \frac{1}{6}, \frac{1}{7}$ **b** $\frac{7}{8}, \frac{5}{6}, \frac{3}{4}, \frac{1}{2}$

   c $\frac{5}{8}, \frac{4}{7}, \frac{2}{3}$ **d** $\frac{7}{11}, \frac{9}{16}, \frac{13}{20}$

13 Copy this number line.

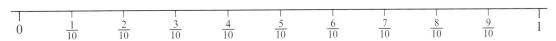

Mark and label the following fractions on the number line as accurately as you can.

   a $\frac{2}{5}$ **b** $\frac{1}{3}$ **c** $\frac{4}{7}$ **d** $\frac{6}{20}$ **e** $\frac{7}{12}$

14 Which number is greater?

   a 0.21 or $\frac{3}{16}$ **b** 0.25 or $\frac{4}{15}$ **c** $\frac{8}{23}$ or 0.36 **d** $\frac{27}{34}$ or 0.78

15 Write each pair of fractions with a common denominator.
Work out the fraction that is exactly halfway between the pairs.

   a $\frac{2}{5}$ and $\frac{4}{9}$ **b** $\frac{3}{5}$ and $\frac{5}{7}$ **c** $\frac{1}{2}$ and $\frac{3}{5}$ **d** $\frac{2}{3}$ and $\frac{7}{8}$

16 Find three fractions between $\frac{2}{9}$ and $\frac{3}{11}$.

Calculations with fractions

- Adding and subtracting fractions with different denominators
- Multiplying and dividing whole numbers by fractions
- Multiplying and dividing fractions by fractions
- Cancelling common factors before multiplying and dividing fractions

Keywords

You should know

explanation 1

1 Work these out, giving each answer in its simplest form.

a $\dfrac{4}{7} + \dfrac{2}{7}$

b $\dfrac{3}{5} - \dfrac{1}{5}$

c $\dfrac{2}{13} + \dfrac{5}{13}$

d $\dfrac{3}{16} + \dfrac{5}{16}$

e $\dfrac{7}{18} - \dfrac{1}{18}$

f $\dfrac{8}{21} - \dfrac{5}{21}$

g $\dfrac{7}{25} + \dfrac{14}{25}$

h $\dfrac{19}{30} - \dfrac{11}{30}$

2 Copy and complete.

$$\dfrac{2}{3} + \dfrac{1}{4} = \dfrac{\square}{12} + \dfrac{\square}{12} = \dfrac{\square + \square}{12} = \dfrac{\square}{12}$$

3 Work these out, giving each answer in its simplest form.

a $\dfrac{1}{5} + \dfrac{7}{10}$

b $\dfrac{3}{8} + \dfrac{1}{4}$

c $\dfrac{3}{7} + \dfrac{5}{14}$

d $\dfrac{7}{12} + \dfrac{1}{6}$

e $\dfrac{4}{14} + \dfrac{1}{42}$

f $\dfrac{16}{32} + \dfrac{4}{8}$

g $\dfrac{3}{13} + \dfrac{5}{39}$

h $\dfrac{7}{9} + \dfrac{1}{81}$

4 Work these out, giving each answer in its simplest form.

a $\dfrac{2}{3} + \dfrac{3}{4}$

b $\dfrac{3}{4} + \dfrac{4}{5}$

c $\dfrac{5}{6} + \dfrac{4}{9}$

d $\dfrac{2}{3} + \dfrac{5}{7}$

e $\dfrac{4}{11} + \dfrac{1}{5}$

f $\dfrac{6}{13} + \dfrac{1}{2}$

g $\dfrac{2}{3} + \dfrac{5}{8}$

h $\dfrac{7}{11} + \dfrac{1}{8}$

5 Copy and complete.

$$\dfrac{3}{4} - \dfrac{2}{5} = \dfrac{\square}{20} - \dfrac{\square}{20} = \dfrac{\square - \square}{20} = \dfrac{\square}{20}$$

6 Work these out, giving each answer in its simplest form.

a $\dfrac{3}{4} - \dfrac{5}{8}$

b $\dfrac{7}{8} - \dfrac{1}{4}$

c $\dfrac{7}{15} - \dfrac{1}{5}$

d $\dfrac{13}{18} - \dfrac{1}{3}$

e $\dfrac{17}{18} - \dfrac{5}{6}$

f $\dfrac{11}{32} - \dfrac{1}{8}$

g $\dfrac{19}{24} - \dfrac{3}{8}$

h $\dfrac{4}{21} - \dfrac{1}{7}$

7 Work these out, giving each answer in its simplest form.

a $\dfrac{8}{9} - \dfrac{1}{2}$

b $\dfrac{3}{5} - \dfrac{1}{4}$

c $\dfrac{7}{8} - \dfrac{2}{3}$

d $\dfrac{5}{6} - \dfrac{3}{4}$

e $\dfrac{11}{18} - \dfrac{5}{12}$

f $\dfrac{6}{7} - \dfrac{2}{5}$

g $\dfrac{4}{9} - \dfrac{2}{7}$

h $\dfrac{11}{19} - \dfrac{1}{3}$

8 Copy and complete this fraction addition square.

+	$\dfrac{1}{2}$	$\dfrac{2}{3}$	
$\dfrac{1}{5}$			
	$\dfrac{3}{4}$		
$\dfrac{2}{7}$			$\dfrac{37}{56}$

explanation 2

9 Copy and complete this fraction addition square.
Remember to simplify your answers.

+	$1\dfrac{1}{3}$	$2\dfrac{1}{3}$	
$\dfrac{2}{5}$			$1\dfrac{1}{3}$
		$\dfrac{1}{2}$	
$2\dfrac{1}{4}$			

10 Although early Egyptians used fractions like $\frac{1}{2}, \frac{1}{3}, \frac{1}{4}$, they did not have notation to write fractions such as $\frac{2}{3}, \frac{4}{5}$ or $\frac{2}{11}$ (though later they used a special symbol for $\frac{2}{3}$).

The fractions they used all had a numerator of one and are called unit fractions. The Egyptians were able to write any fraction as a sum of unit fractions.

For example, $\frac{3}{8} = \frac{1}{4} + \frac{1}{8}$ $\frac{5}{12} = \frac{1}{4} + \frac{1}{6}$ $\frac{7}{9} = \frac{1}{2} + \frac{1}{4} + \frac{1}{36}$

Write these fractions as Egyptian fractions (do not use the same denominator for all your Egyptian fractions).

Some can be done in more than one way!

a $\frac{5}{8}$ b $\frac{7}{12}$ c $\frac{13}{15}$

d $\frac{9}{20}$ e $\frac{17}{30}$

explanation 3a   explanation 3b

11 Work these out.

a $\frac{2}{3}$ of 16   b $\frac{2}{5}$ of £240   c $\frac{3}{8}$ of 150 g

d $\frac{4}{7}$ of 50 kg   e three quarters of 75   f five ninths of 30

g $\frac{5}{12}$ of 100 cm   h $\frac{5}{6}$ of 40p   i $\frac{7}{8}$ of 140 m

12 Two of the answers in each set will be the same. Find each odd one out.

a i $\frac{3}{4}$ of 64   ii $\frac{7}{11} \times 77$ iii $\frac{3}{5}$ of 80

b i $\frac{5}{8}$ of 48   ii $\frac{4}{7}$ of 56   iii one third of 96

13 This pie chart shows the colours of 80 cars in a car park.

    a $\frac{1}{4}$ of the cars are silver.

        How many silver cars are there?

    b $\frac{3}{8}$ of the cars are red.

        How many red cars are there?

    c There are 12 black cars.

        What fraction of the total number of cars is this?

    d How many blue cars are there?

    e What fraction of the cars are blue?

    f The sum of the angles at the centre of the pie chart is 360°.

        Find the angle for each sector.

14 Work these out.

    a $\frac{2}{5} \times 14$ **b** $\frac{4}{9} \times 24$ **c** $\frac{3}{5} \times 16$ **d** $\frac{4}{6} \times 32$

    e $\frac{3}{8} \times 14$ **f** $\frac{5}{16} \times 9$ **g** $\frac{7}{9} \times 36$ **h** $\frac{1}{35} \times 14$

15 Work these out.

    a $\frac{5}{6} \times 42\,\text{kg}$ **b** $\frac{7}{12} \times 11\,\text{kg}$ **c** $\frac{5}{3} \times 26\,\text{cm}$ **d** $\frac{9}{5} \times 120\,\text{g}$

    e $\frac{6}{7} \times 15\,\text{m}$ **f** $\frac{7}{9} \times 21$ seconds   **g** $\frac{3}{11} \times 17\,\text{ml}$ **h** $\frac{4}{5} \times £84$

16 Copy and complete this grid.

$\frac{2}{5}$	×	80	=	
×	■	×	■	×
105	×	$\frac{3}{10}$	=	
=	■	=	■	=
	×		=	

explanation 4a   explanation 4b

17 Write the reciprocal of each number.

    a 5   **b** 7   **c** 10   **d** $\frac{1}{4}$ **e** $\frac{1}{8}$ **f** $\frac{1}{25}$

18 **a** How many sevenths are there in this rectangle?

    b How many thirds of a circle are there in these four circles?

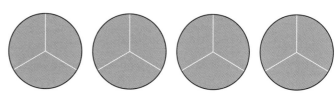

    c How many sixths of a prism are there in these three prisms?

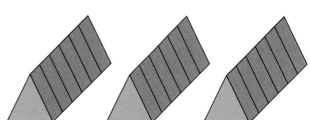

19 Copy and complete this sentence.

Dividing by $\frac{1}{5}$ is the same as multiplying by $\square$.

20 Work these out.

    a $10 \div \frac{1}{2}$ **b** $9 \div \frac{1}{3}$ **c** $12 \div \frac{1}{5}$ **d** $20 \div \frac{1}{7}$

    e $8 \div \frac{1}{4}$ **f** $15 \div \frac{1}{6}$ **g** $3 \div \frac{1}{10}$ **h** $1 \div \frac{1}{12}$

21 Copy and complete these number sentences.

    a $30 \times \frac{1}{5} = \square$ therefore $\square \div \frac{1}{5} = 30$ and $\square \div 30 = \frac{1}{5}$

    b $15 \times \frac{2}{5} = \square$ therefore $\square \div \frac{2}{5} = 15$ and $\square \div 15 = \frac{2}{5}$

    c $\square \times \frac{3}{5} = 6$ therefore $6 \div \frac{3}{5} = \square$ and $6 \div \square = \frac{3}{5}$

    d $\square \times \frac{4}{5} = 6$ therefore $6 \div \frac{4}{5} = \square$ and $6 \div \square = \frac{4}{5}$

22 Your answers to question **21** will help you answer these questions.

   a When you multiply a positive number by a fraction less than one is the answer a smaller or larger number than the first one?

   b When you divide a positive number by a fraction less than one is the answer a smaller or larger number than the first one?

> explanation 5

23 The diagram shows a 4 × 7 grid of squares.

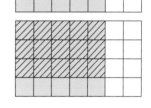

   a What fraction of the diagram is coloured blue?

      Give your answer in its simplest form.

   b What fraction of the blue squares are now shaded?

      Give your answer in its simplest form.

   c What fraction of the whole diagram is shaded?

   d Use your answers to parts **a**, **b** and **c** to complete

$$\frac{\square}{\square} \times \frac{\square}{\square} = \frac{\square}{\square}$$

24 Work these out.

   a $\dfrac{3}{8} \times \dfrac{7}{10}$ **b** $\dfrac{9}{11} \times \dfrac{4}{5}$ **c** $\dfrac{8}{15} \times \dfrac{2}{3}$

25 Work these out.

   a $\dfrac{9}{16} \times \dfrac{24}{25}$ **b** $\dfrac{11}{12} \times \dfrac{8}{33}$ **c** $\dfrac{21}{25} \times \dfrac{5}{14}$

26 In a survey, three-quarters of pupils said that they walk to school and two-thirds of these said that they regularly have a school dinner.

   a What fraction of the pupils in the survey walk to school and regularly have a school dinner? Show your calculation.

   b Which pupils are represented by the calculation $\dfrac{3}{4} \times \dfrac{1}{3}$?

27 For any input value these two function machines give the same output value.

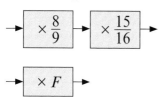

a Write F as a fraction in its lowest terms.

b What is the output when the input value is $\frac{4}{15}$?

---

explanation 6 ━━━━━━━━━━━━━━━━━━━━━━━━━━━━━━━━━━━━━━

28 Copy and complete.

$$24 \div \frac{12}{25} = 24 \times \frac{\square}{\square}$$

$$= \square$$

29 Work these out.

a $32 \div \frac{8}{9}$ **b** $24 \div \frac{16}{3}$ **c** $12 \div \frac{18}{5}$

30 A large drill rotates once every $\frac{3}{4}$ second.

How many times will the drill rotate in one minute?

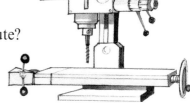

31 Work these out.

a $\frac{2}{9} \div \frac{3}{4}$ **b** $\frac{1}{4} \div \frac{7}{8}$ **c** $\frac{5}{12} \div \frac{25}{24}$

32 A contractor has a budget of £$\frac{3}{4}$ million to cover all production costs on a project.

The production costs work out at £50 000 per month.

a Write £50 000 as a fraction of £$\frac{3}{4}$ million.

b How many months production can be paid for from the budget?

Percentages

- Calculating percentages of numbers, quantities and measurements
- Using percentages to solve problems
- Finding the outcome of a percentage increase or decrease
- Calculating successive percentage increases or decreases

Keywords

You should know

explanation 1

1 Copy and complete the table.

	Fraction	Decimal	Percentage
a	$\dfrac{1}{4}$		
b		0.54	
c			16%
d	$\dfrac{1}{3}$		
e		0.625	
f			81%
g			4%

2 Write each percentage as a fraction in its simplest form.

   a 72%   **b** 98%   **c** 45%   **d** 3%   **e** 12.5%

3 Write each decimal as a percentage.

   a 0.69   **b** 0.05   **c** 0.485   **d** 1.64   **e** 3.516

4 Molly asked 60 pupils to name their favourite flavour of crisp.
Her results are in this table.

Plain	Cheese and onion	Salt and vinegar	BBQ	Prawn cocktail
4	15	8	21	12

a 21 out of the 60 pupils chose **BBQ** flavour.

This can be written as a fraction $\frac{21}{60} = \frac{7}{20}$.

What fraction of the group chose each of
the other flavours?

b What percentage of the group chose each
flavour?

explanation 2a   explanation 2b

5 Work out these percentages.

   a 15% of 24   **b** 33% of 12   **c** 35% of 40

   d 75% of 42   **e** 44% of 75   **f** 57% of 80

6 Find these amounts.

   a 37% of 84 kg   **b** 18% of £72   **c** 2.9% of 51 km

   d 32.6% of 28 m   **e** 120% of £32   **f** 105% of 47 kg

   g 123% of 27 litres   **h** 0.4% of 13 tonnes   **i** 112.5% of 65 cm

7 Work out these amounts, rounding each answer to the nearest penny.

   a 46% of £21   **b** 33% of £52   **c** $18\frac{1}{4}$% of £65

8 Peter puts £200 into a bank account that pays 4.5% interest.

   a How much interest will he receive after
one year?

   b How much will he now have in the account?

9 20% of this piece of fabric is green. What area of the fabric is green?

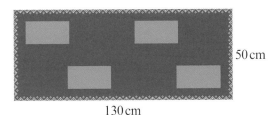

50 cm

130 cm

10

The pie chart shows how pupils in a class travel to school.
If 30 pupils travel by car, how many walk to school?

explanation 3

11 Work out these percentages.

a   45 as a percentage of 60

b   15 as a percentage of 75

c   32 as a percentage of 128

d   42 as a percentage of 112

12 The human body consists of 206 bones.
There are 26 bones in each foot.
What percentage of the bones in the
human skeleton are in the feet?

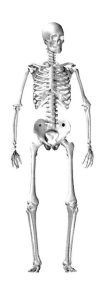

13 Steve's test scores are given in the table.

Subject	English	Maths	Geography	History	Science
Score	$\frac{35}{40}$	$\frac{80}{90}$	$\frac{28}{35}$	$\frac{54}{60}$	$\frac{56}{64}$
Percentage					

   a Copy and complete the table by working out Steve's percentage score for each subject.

   b In which subject did Steve achieve his best result?

14 Work out these percentages.
Give your answers to 1 decimal place.

   a 40p as a percentage of £5   **b** 20 minutes as a percentage of 4 hours

   c 35 g as a percentage of 1.5 kg   **d** 62 cm as a percentage of 2.8 m

15 Sophie puts £250 into her savings account.
After one year she receives £8.75 in interest.
What was the rate of interest paid on her savings?

explanation 4

16 Each price is increased by the percentage shown.

Calculate the new values.

   a £30 is increased by 15%   **b** £65 is increased by 12%

   c £82 is increased by 3%   **d** £16 is increased by 45.6%

   e £124 is increased by 132%   **f** £240 is increased by 0.5%

17 Electricity prices go up by 11%.
Find the new cost of electricity that originally cost these amounts.

   a £70   **b** £360   **c** £470   **d** £550

18 Council tax bills are increased by 4% this year.

a Copy and complete this statement.

This year's council tax bill will be ☐% of last year's bill.

☐% is equivalent to ☐.☐.

b How much will the council tax be this year if it was this much last year?

   i £800   ii £1050   iii £1720

19 £2020 was raised at the school fair last year.

a This year the amount raised was 8% more than last year.
How much money was raised this year?

b 5% of the amount raised last year came from the ice-cream stall.
How much money did it take?

20 In 1994 Martin and Susie bought a house for £150 000 and a year later its value had increased by 4.5%.

a What was the value of their house after the increase?

b The following year its value increased by another 4.5%.
What was its value then?

21 Last year at Albany Community school 67.5% of pupils passed their end of year exams

a This year 204 pupils out of 296 passed their exams.
Has the school's percentage changed? If so, by what percentage has it increased or decreased?

b If the school had 280 candidates for the exams last year, how many of them passed?

explanation 5

22 Each price is reduced by the percentage shown. Calculate the new values.

a £65 is reduced by 65%

b £98 is reduced by 77%

c £456 is reduced by 21%

23 A reduction of 5% is given if a customer buys gas and electricity from the same supplier. The total bill for gas and electricity is £784 before the discount is applied. How much will the customer actually pay?

24 Tom wants to buy a car which costs £5600. He can either pay the total in cash or pay a 20% deposit followed by 24 equal monthly payments of £190. How much extra will Tom pay using the second method?

explanation 6

25 House prices increased by 4% in June 2007. In November it was reported that house prices had fallen by 4% since June. A house was valued at £240 000 in May. Work out the value of that house at the start of December 2007.

26 Karan keeps koi carp.

His biggest fish weighed 7 kg before it got carp pox (CHV-1) and began to lose weight at 5% per day.

However, after a week it started to recover and gained weight at 8% per day.

a What did it weigh the day after it got carp pox?

b What did it weigh a week after it got carp pox?

c How many days after it got carp pox did it regain its 7 kg weight?

27 a In 2007 an energy report said that the wind industry generated 1% of the world's electricity and that if generation of wind power grew by 20% per year for 15 years, it would still only generate 10% of the world's electricity. Is this a true claim?

b The report also said that solar energy contributed only 0.06% of world electricity and that if generation of solar energy increased by 35% per year, it would still generate less than 5% of world electricity in 15 years. Is this a true claim?

Mental methods (1)

- Using facts you know to answer unfamiliar questions
- Working with multiples, factors, powers and roots

Keywords

You should know

Answer the questions in this section without using a calculator, unless told otherwise.

explanation 1a | explanation 1b

1 Write these fractions as decimals.

a $\dfrac{1}{5}$

b $\dfrac{3}{4}$

c $\dfrac{7}{20}$

d $\dfrac{6}{25}$

e $\dfrac{3}{8}$

f $\dfrac{4}{5}$

g $\dfrac{5}{8}$

h $\dfrac{9}{10}$

i $\dfrac{7}{50}$

2 a i Use the fact that $\dfrac{1}{8} = 0.125$ to write $\dfrac{3}{8}$ as a decimal.

ii Check your answer to part **i** by calculating $3 \div 8$.

iii What is $\dfrac{7}{8}$ as a decimal?

How did you work it out?

Explain another method you could have used.

b Use the fact that $\dfrac{1}{8} = 0.125$ to work out these fractions.

i $\dfrac{1}{80}$

ii $\dfrac{1}{16}$

iii $\dfrac{1}{40}$

iv $\dfrac{3}{16}$

3 Write these decimals as fractions.
Give each answer in its simplest form.

a 0.4

b 0.85

c 0.84

d 0.625

e 1.9

f 2.375

g 3.72

h 4.44

i 10.16

4 Group these cards into sets so that each set contains an equivalent fraction, decimal and percentage.

Some cards are missing.

Work out what should be on the missing cards to complete the sets.

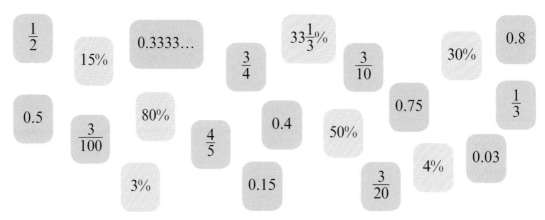

5 Rewrite each article using percentages where appropriate.

a The chocolate digestive is Britain's favourite biscuit. The chocolate hobnob came second in a poll of 5000 people. About a third of people in the UK eat biscuits as a mid-morning snack but the largest proportion, four out of ten, eat them as they watch TV.

b Nine out of ten people say that parents should be told if their children are obese. More than $\frac{7}{10}$ said the government should abandon its plan to allow parents to opt out of being told. The poll used a research panel of a hundred families, each of two adults and up to four children.

explanation 2a   explanation 2b

6 Work out these quantities.

a 15% of £38	**b** 35% of 72 kg	**c** 21% of £62	**d** 30% of £56
e 64% of 39 km	**f** $33\frac{1}{3}$% of 69 m	**g** 5% of £20	**h** 3% of 15 km

7 This table gives details of the first week's viewing figures for a television programme over a 3-year period.

Work out estimates for the audience in each year.

Year	2008	2007	2006
% of total TV audience	19.9%	24.8%	33.4%
Estimated total TV audience in millions	20.5	20.0	21.6
Estimated programme audience in millions			

8 The prices shown do not include VAT.

£200   £550   £120

a Work out the VAT, at a rate of 17.5%, for each item.

b Find the total cost of each item, including VAT.

9 These are the normal prices of some items.
In a sale all items are reduced by 15%. Find the sale prices.

a trainers costing £45

b tennis racquet costing £38

c football costing £16

d hockey stick costing £55

e mountain bike costing £160

f table-tennis ball costing 60p

10 **a** **i** Find 25% of 10% of £800

        ii Now work out 10% of 25% of £800

    b **i** Find 50% of 5% of £800

        ii Now work out 5% of 50% of £800

    c **i** Find 10% of 50% of £400

        ii Now work out 50% of 10% of £400

    d Write a sentence explaining what you notice about your answers to **a**, **b** and **c**.

explanation 3a   explanation 3b

11 Copy and complete this table.

3	×	4	=	
2	×	4	=	
1	×	4	=	
0.1	×	4	=	
0.2	×	4	=	
0.3	×	4	=	

12 Use the fact that $8 \times 4 = 32$ to work out these products.

    a 8×0.4 **b** 0.8×0.4 **c** 80×0.4

    d 8×0.04 **e** 80×40 **f** 0.8×400

13 Use the fact that $9 \times 7 = 63$ to work out these products.

    a 0.9×7 **b** 9×0.7 **c** 90×7

    d 90×0.7 **e** 0.09×0.7 **f** 900×0.7

14 Use your answer to part **a** to work out the answers to parts **b**, **c** and **d**.

    a $20 \div 4$ **b** $2 \div 4$ **c** $0.2 \div 4$ **d** $0.02 \div 4$

15 Use your answer to part **a** to work out the answers to parts **b**, **c** and **d**.

    a $18 \div 2$ **b** $1.8 \div 2$ **c** $0.18 \div 2$ **d** $0.018 \div 2$

16 Copy and complete these statements. Do not use the number 1!

   a $\square \times \square = 6$ **b** $\square \times \square = 0.8$

   c $\square \times \square = 0.4$ **d** $\square \div \square = 3$

   e $\square \div \square = 0.2$ **f** $\square \div \square = 0.5$

17 Make 36 using the digits 1, 3 , 3 and 5 once each, together with any combination of the symbols $+$, $-$, $\times$, $\div$ and brackets.

18 Andy was born in 1982. Using the digits of that year, in any order, together with any combination of the symbols $+$, $-$, $\times$, $\div$ and brackets, how many numbers between 1 and 30 can you make?

19 To multiply a number by 25 Ann multiplies by 5 then by 5 again.

   Bushra multiplies by 100 then divides by 4.

   Connie halves the number twice then moves the digits two places to the left.

   Explain why each pupil has a correct method.

20 Copy and complete this table of squares and cubes.

Number (x)	1	2	3	4	5	6	7	8	9	10
Square (x^2)	1		9							
Cube (x^3)	1			64						

21 In 1770 Joseph Louis Lagrange, a French mathematician, proved that every whole number can be expressed as the sum of no more than four squares. For example

   $31 = 5^2 + 2^2 + 1^2 + 1^2$

   $21 = 4^2 + 2^2 + 1^2$

   a Using your table from question **20** to help you, show that this is true for all the whole numbers from 80 to 90 inclusive.

   b Which of the numbers in part **a** can you make in more than one way?

22 Find those multiples of 5 less than 100 that can be expressed as the sum or difference of two squares. Use your table from question **20** to help you.

explanation 4

23 Split the numbers into factors to help work out these products.

a 16×25 b 75×28 c 35×8

d $64 \times 125 \times 15$ e $425 \div 25$ f $462 \div 14$

24 Square roots of large numbers can sometimes be found by splitting the number into factors.

$\sqrt{225} = \sqrt{9 \times 25} = \sqrt{9} \times \sqrt{25} = 3 \times 5 = 15$

Work these out by splitting each number into factors that are square numbers.

a $\sqrt{324}$ b $\sqrt{900}$ c $\sqrt{729}$

d $\sqrt{196}$ e $\sqrt{2500}$ f $\sqrt{1225}$

explanation 5

25 Change just one digit in each number to make it a multiple of 9.

a   367   b   12 345   c   62 628   d   22 222

26 Change just one digit in each number to make it a multiple of 9 and 5.

a   365   b   27 280   c   62 025   d   48 102

27

35 875   4 283 604

24 255   5 377 779

160 600

a   Which of these numbers are multiples of 5?

b   Which of these numbers are multiples of 9?

Simplifying expressions

- Simplifying expressions by collecting like terms
- Expanding expressions involving brackets
- Writing expressions using index notation
- The order of operations for expressions involving indices

Keywords

You should know

explanation 1a   explanation 1b   explanation 1c

1 Look at the terms in the box.

$$5xy \quad 6x \quad -7x^2 \quad 4y \quad -1$$
$$4x \quad 9 \quad -10y \quad -yx \quad xy^2$$

Write down all the terms in the box that are like each term below.

a $2x$ **b** $-3xy$ **c** $2x^2$ **d** -8 **e** y **f** y^2

2 Simplify these expressions where possible. Collect like terms.

a $4h + t - 3h + 5t$

b $a + 8b + 10 + 5a - 3$

c $5m - 3n + 8 - m + n + 1 + n$

d $3q + 8 - p + 3 - 6q - 11 + 2p$

e $m + 6n - m + n - 5 + 6n + 3m$

f $x - 7y + y^2 - 3 - 2x^2 + 6z$

g $-a + 7b - ab + 4ab - b + 1$

h $2m - 3n + 2 - m + n + 1 + 2n$

3 Write three different expressions that simplify to $3x + 7y - 6$.

4 Eric has three rectangular cards. One of them has a hole cut out.

a Write down an expression for the area of each card.

b What is the total area of the three cards? Simplify your answer.

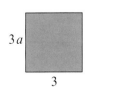

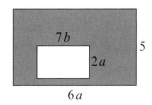

5 Copy and complete the expressions.

   a $5a + b + 4 - \Box + 6b + \Box = 3a + \Box + 5$

   b $4t - u + t - v - \Box = \Box - 9u - v$

   c $p + 7q - 7 - q + \Box - \Box = 12p + \Box - 8$

   d $a + 3b - 2 + 4a - \Box + 1 = \Box - 3b - \Box$

   e $-v - 3 + 2w + 1 + \Box - \Box = 3v + \Box - 6$

   f $2x + y - 3 + 5x - \Box + \Box = 7x + 6$

6 Simplify these expressions.

   a $5x^2 + y^2 - 2x + y - x^2 - 8y^2 + x + 4y$

   b $x^2 + 5y^2 - 5 + x + 3 - 4x^2 + 5x - 10$

   c $4x - 8y + 2xy - x + 5y - 7x - 8yx + 3x$

   d $5x + y^2 - 2x + y - x^2 - 8y^2 + x + 4y$

   e $6a + b - 4ab + 2a + 7ba - 10b + 2$

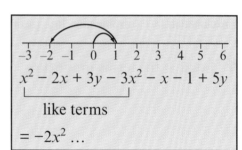

$x^2 - 2x + 3y - 3x^2 - x - 1 + 5y$

like terms

$= -2x^2 \ldots$

7 Write three different expressions that simplify to $2x^2 - 3x + 9$.

8 Write an expression for the perimeter of each shape as simply as possible.

   a

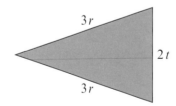

   b

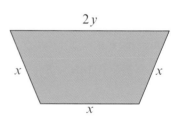

   c

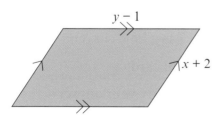

   d

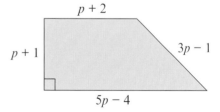

explanation 2a | explanation 2b

9 Expand the brackets.

a $3(2a + b)$ **b** $5(m - 6n)$ **c** $2(x - 3y)$ **d** $12(4a + 3b)$

e $a(3a + 4)$ **f** $x(10 - x)$ **g** $p(q - 7p - 1)$ **h** $y(1 - 4y - 3x)$

i $4t(2 - 5t)$ **j** $8u(3u - 10)$ **k** $9v(u - 2v + 4)$ **l** $3x(2 + 6x - 7x^2)$

10 Expand the brackets and simplify where possible.

a $5(x - 2y) + 3xy$

b $4(a + 2b) - 3a$

c $8(3a - b) + 2(4a + 3b)$

d $6(a + 2b) + 4(a - 5b)$

e $9(2 - b) + (7 - b)$

f $x(x - y) + y(x - y)$

explanation 3

11 Expand the brackets.

a $-2(3 - 5t)$

b $-4(3 + 5t)$

c $-y(3y - 10)$

d $-p(2q - 5p)$

e $-x(1 - x)$

f $-a(2a - b + 3)$

g $-8n(2 - m + 3n)$

h $-5m(2 + 7m - m^2)$

$$-3(1 - 2x)$$
$$= -3 \times 1 + (-3) \times (-2x)$$
$$= -3 + 6x$$

12 Expand the brackets and simplify.

a $2(3x + 1) - 5(x + 1)$

b $10a - 3(2a + 5b)$

c $2a - (4a - 3b)$

d $6 - (2t - 1)$

e $2(3m - n) - (4m + 3n)$

f $4a(2a + 1) - 3a(a - 2)$

g $2(4x + y) + 3(2x - 9y)$

h $5a(a - 3) - a(2a + 7)$

13 Aled has 13 CDs. Beth has $3y$ fewer CDs than Aled. Ciaran has $7xy$ CDs.

a How many CDs do Aled and Beth have altogether?

b For each CD that Aled and Beth have, Ciaran gives them another $2x$ CDs.

i How many CDs does Ciaran give them?

ii How many CDs does Ciaran have left? Simplify your expression.

14 Copy and complete.

a $\Box(3-2t)=15-\Box$

b $4(7+\Box)=\Box+12b$

c $8(\Box+\Box)=8x+24y$

d $\Box(2-5t)=6t-\Box$

e $\Box(x-6)=2x^2-\Box$

f $\Box(n-2m)=n^2-\Box$

g $\Box(2x-7)=-8x+\Box$

h $\Box(4x-3)=\Box+15x$

i $\Box(m+6n)=\Box-6mn$

j $\Box(x-3y)=\Box+6y$

15 The area of a rectangle is $(2x^2+4x)\,\text{cm}^2$

Find its length and width for each of these perimeters.

a $(6x+8)$ cm   b $(6x+4)$ cm

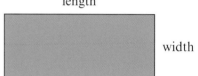

length

width

explanation 4a   explanation 4b

16 Write these expressions as simply as possible using index notation.

a $y\times y\times y$

b $r\times r\times r\times r$

c $p\times p\times p\times p\times p$

d $t\times t\times u\times u\times u$

e $y\times y\times y\times z$

f $a\times a\times b\times b\times c\times c$

g $m\times n\times n\times p\times p\times p$

h $t\times u\times t\times u\times t$

i $m\times p\times n\times m\times p$

17 Write these in full. The first one has been done for you.

a $t^2=t\times t$

b f^2g

c b^3d^2

d y^4z^3

e $a^2b^2c^3$

f mn^3p^2

18 a Write these in full.

i $y^2\times y^3$

ii $a\times a^5$

iii $p^3\times p\times p^2$

b Write the expressions in part **a** as simply as possible using index notation.

c Copy and complete these expressions. Use your answers to part **b** to help.

i $x^n\times x^m=x^\Box$

ii $z\times z^k=z^\Box$

iii $q^a\times q^b\times q=q^\Box$

19 Simplify.

   a $2 \times a \times 3 \times a \times 4 \times a$ **b** $7 \times a \times 2 \times a \times a \times a$

   c $2 \times n \times n \times m \times n \times m$ **d** $5 \times n \times m \times n \times m \times m \times 3$

   e $6 \times y^3 \times 2 \times y$ **f** $2 \times m \times m \times 6 \times n \times m^2 \times 4 \times m$

20 Complete these expressions so that they all simplify to $30t^2u^3v$.

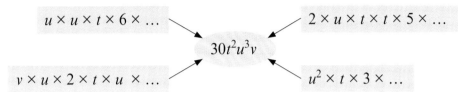

$u \times u \times t \times 6 \times \ldots$ $2 \times u \times t \times t \times 5 \times \ldots$

$$30t^2u^3v$$

$v \times u \times 2 \times t \times u \times \ldots$ $u^2 \times t \times 3 \times \ldots$

| explanation 5a | explanation 5b | explanation 5c |

21 $m = 4$ and $v = 5$. Work out the value of each expression.
Which expressions have the same value?

   $30 - 2v$ $(3m)^2$ $2m^2 - 12$ $(v - m)(v + m)$ $2vm^2$

      $4 + 3mv$ $v^2 - m^2$ $3(30 - mv)$ $8(v^2 - 5)$

22 Which values of n make each algebraic expression equal to 18?

   In each case, n is a positive whole number less than 10.

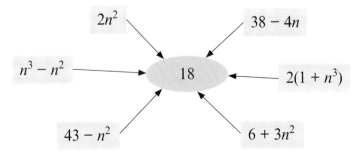

$2n^2$ $38 - 4n$

$n^3 - n^2$ 18 $2(1 + n^3)$

$43 - n^2$ $6 + 3n^2$

23 Look at this statement.

   $(p + q)^2 = p^2 + q^2$

   Is the statement always true, never true or sometimes true?

   Use different values of p and q to explain your answer.

Using equations

- How to solve equations involving brackets
- How to form and solve simple equations

Keywords

You should know

explanation 1a | explanation 1b | explanation 1c | explanation 1d

1 Solve these equations.

a $2n = 6$

b $3p + 1 = 4$

c $5y - 2 = 13$

d $3x - 2 = 16$

e $8 = 12a - 4$

f $22 = 6b - 8$

g $12 + 4p = 4$

h $6a + 1 = -5$

i $5d - 4 = -19$

2 Each table gives instructions for solving an equation. Copy and complete.

a Solve $5x - 2 = 3x + 9$

Action to both sides	Effect
$- 3x$	$2x - 2 = 9$
$+ 2$	$2x = 11$
$\div 2$	

b Solve $x - 3 = 7x - 15$

Action to both sides	Effect
$- x$	
$+ 15$	
$\div 6$	

c Solve $12k + 7 = 2k$

Action to both sides	Effect
$- 2k$	
$- 7$	
$\div 10$	

d Solve $\dfrac{p}{2} + 9 = 3p$

Action to both sides	Effect
$\times 2$	
$- p$	
$\div 5$	

3 Solve these equations using a method similar to question **2**.

a $8x - 19 = 5x + 2$

b $6a - 7 = 2a + 13$

c $3x - 4 = 10x - 25$

d $7x - 2 = 10x - 5$

e $2 + 8x = 5x + 8$

f $7k - 3 = 5k - 6$

4

How do I solve $24 = 9 - 3m$?

Add $3m$ to both sides first to make the m positive. Then try to solve the equation.

    a Follow Jane's advice and solve $24 = 9 - 3m$.

    b Explain how to solve $30 - 10p = 9$.

5 Solve these equations.

    a $x = 12 - 3x$ **b** $5 - 2n = n + 17$ **c** $12 - m = 17 - 11m$

> explanation 2a   explanation 2b   explanation 2c

6 Solve these equations.

    a $2(x + 1) = 6$ **b** $5(m - 2) = 15$ **c** $5 = 2(a - 1)$

    d $4(p - 6) = 0$ **e** $3(y + 6) - 24 = 0$ **f** $2(z + 1) + 3 = 5$

    g $\dfrac{x + 1}{2} = 3$ **h** $\dfrac{8}{b} = 4$ **i** $5 + \dfrac{8}{c} = 21$

    j $4 - \dfrac{9}{k} = 7$ **k** $\dfrac{3}{p} + 4 = 0$ **l** $\dfrac{25}{g} = g$

7 Copy and complete the table to solve the equation $-3 = \dfrac{1 + q}{1 - q}$.

Action to both sides	Effect
Multiply by $(1 - q)$	
Subtract q	
Add 3	
Divide by 2	

8

How do I solve $6(2y - 1) - (8y - 3) = 21$?

Collect like terms. But first check the second line.

$6(2y - 1) - (8y - 3) = 21$
$\rightarrow 12y - 6 - 8y - 3 = 21$
one mistake

a What error has Ellie made in her second line? Complete the solution for her.

b Solve $3(4n - 1) - 2(2n - 7) = 51$.

9 Solve each equation. Use a method similar to questions **8**.

a $5(x - 4) + 3(x + 12) = 0$

b $8 + 4(2x + 5) = x$

c $3(x + 2) - (x - 1) = 8$

d $7(x - 1) - 2(x - 3) = 14$

e $3(2x - 3) + 2(1 - 2x) = 6$

f $9x + 14 = 2(3x + 8)$

g $5(1 - 3x) = 4(2 - 3x)$

h $5(x - 1) = 3(x + 5)$

explanation 3a   explanation 3b

10 Brian, Keith and Nadeem each write an expression on a piece of card.

$2(3x + 5)$
Brian

$10(x + 2)$
Keith

$2x - 39$
Nadeem

a What value of x makes the value of Brian's card equal to Keith's card?

b Find the value of x that makes the sum of all these cards equal to zero.

11 A logo is made by placing four identical triangles together.

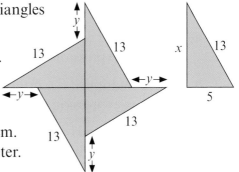

a Write an expression for y in terms of x.

b Write an expression for the perimeter of the logo. Simplify it.

c The actual perimeter of the logo is 80 cm. Write down an equation for the perimeter. Solve it to find x.

12 Handmade chocolates are arranged on a three-tier tray. The top tray contains 10 fewer chocolates than the middle tray. The bottom tray contains 3 times as many as the top tray.

Let x be the number of chocolates on the middle tray.

a Write the number of chocolates on the top tray in terms of x.

b How many chocolates are on the bottom tray? Give your answer in terms of x.

c There are 70 chocolates altogether. Write an equation and solve it to find x.

d How many chocolates are there on each tray?

13 At the start of a game, Peter and Sheila had 70 marbles altogether. They played a game and Peter lost 10 marbles to Sheila.

Let m be the number of marbles Peter had at the start.

a Copy and complete the table.

	Peter	Sheila
Number of marbles at the start of the game	m	
Number of marbles at the end of the game		

b At the end of the game, Sheila had four times as many marbles as Peter. Write an equation, in terms of m, to show this. Solve it to find the value of m.

c How many marbles did Peter have at the end of the game?

14 Mrs Logan wrote a negative number on the board. She called the number n.

   a Sarah added 3 to the number, and then multiplied her answer by 8.
   Write an expression for her result.

   b David multiplied the original number by 6, and then added 2.
   Write an expression for his result.

   c Sarah and David got the same final answer. Use your answers to parts **a**
   and **b** to write an equation. Solve it to find the value of n.

15 David and Julie had 60 minutes of call time altogether.
They each phoned a friend. David used 1 minute and Julie used 4 minutes.
David then had four times as much call time as Julie had.

Let t be the number of minutes David had
before he phoned his friend.

   a Copy and complete the table.

	David	Julie
Number of minutes before call	t	
Number of minutes remaining after call		

   b Write an equation and solve it to find t.

16 A barrel contained 11 litres of water. Another barrel contained 3 litres of
water. Linda added x litres of water to both barrels. The first barrel then had
three times as much water as the second barrel had.

   a Draw and complete a table, like that in question **15**.

   b Write an equation in terms of x.

   c Solve your equation to find the value of x.
   How much water was in each barrel after Linda added the extra water?

17 At the start of their holiday, Christine and Gavin had $120 altogether.
At the airport, their aunt gave them another $21 each.
Gavin then had twice as much as Christine.

Let *x* represent the amount Christine had before her aunt gave her $21.

a Copy and complete the table.

	Christine	Gavin
At the start of the holiday	*x*	
At the airport		

b Write an equation and solve it to find *x*.

c How much money did Gavin have at the airport?

18 Write an equation for each shape and solve it.

a

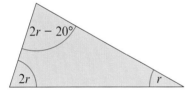

b

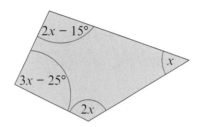

c

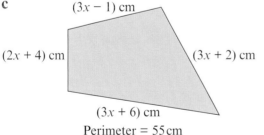

Perimeter = 55 cm

d

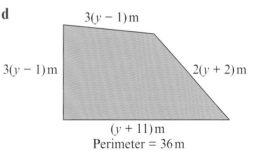

Perimeter = 36 m

e

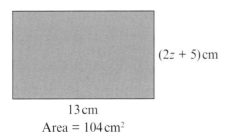

Area = 104 cm²

f

Area = 1960 m²

Formulae

- Finding the value of a formula
- Obtaining a formula
- Checking that a formula works

Keywords

You should know

explanation 1

1 Fatima thinks 7^2 is 14. What mistake has she made?

2 Sam has made mistakes. Copy his work out correctly.
Explain how each calculation should be done.

$$
\begin{array}{lll}
\text{a} \quad 2 \times 5^2 = 100 \; \text{✗} & \text{b} \quad 2^3 = 6 \; \text{✗} & \text{c} \quad 1^2 = 2 \; \text{✗} \\
\text{d} \quad 3^2 + 4^2 = 49 \; \text{✗} & \text{e} \quad (-3)^2 = -9 \; \text{✗} & \text{f} \quad (-2)^3 = 8 \; \text{✗}
\end{array}
$$

3 Which cards match each other? (Some of the cards will be left over.)

8^2 $5x^2 + 3x^2$ $15x^4$ x^{10} $8x^4$ 8×8 x^3

x^2 $x \times x^2$ 64 $x^7 \times x^3$ $x^m \times x^n$ $8x^2$ $x \times x$

16 $x + x$ $x + x^2$ $2x$ $5x^2 \times 3x^2$ x^{m+n} x^{21}

explanation 2a   explanation 2b

4 $R = 3$, $S = 2$ and $T = -4$. Find the value of each expression.

a R^2 b $10R^2$ c $1 + R^3$ d $5 + 3S^3$

e $R^3 - 4S^3$ f T^3 g $2T^2$ h S^2T^3

5 $a = 3$, $b = 4$ and $c = 10$. Which envelope contains the value of each expression?

A 43	B −6	C 18
D 34	E 1	F −7
G 54	H 36	I 28
J 405	K 2	L 8.5

a $2(a + b - c)$ **b** $a^2 b$ **c** $10 - a^2$

d $5(c - 1)^2$ **e** $2ab + c$ **f** $a(b^2 - c)$

g $a^2 - b^2$ **h** $\dfrac{b + c}{a + b}$ **i** $(a - 1)(b - 1)(c - 1)$

j $\dfrac{a + b + c}{2}$ **k** $3 + bc$

6 One envelope in question **5** was not used.
Make up three different expressions that could go inside this envelope.

7 $u = 4$, $v = 2$ and $w = -3$. Find the value of each expression.

a $u + w$ **b** $u - w$ **c** $u^2 + 6v^2$

d $u^3 + v^3$ **e** uv^3 **f** $2(v - w)^2$

g $5wv^2$ **h** $2w^3$ **i** $7 - 2vw$

j $(u + 2w)^3$ **k** $(v^3 - w^2)(2u + v)$ **l** $(v + w)(u + v)^2$

8 $p = 5$, $q = 6$ and $r = -2$. Find the value of each expression.

a $5p - 2q$ **b** $2p + 3r$ **c** $2q^2 + 5r^2$

d $8p^2 + 1$ **e** $\dfrac{26 + r^3}{p + q + r}$ **f** $4r^3 + 7$

g $2p^2 - 3r$ **h** $10q^2 - 7$ **i** $2p^3 - 6p$

explanation 3a explanation 3b

9 A rectangle has length l and width w.
This is the formula for c, the number of squares
that are cut by a diagonal of the rectangle.

$c = l + w - (\text{HCF of } l \text{ and } w)$

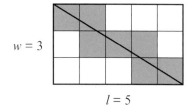

$w = 3$

$l = 5$

a   Paul checks the formula on a 5 by 3 rectangle. He shades the squares that
have been cut by the diagonal and counts them. The answer is $c = 7$.
Does the formula give the same answer?

b   Draw rectangles for these values of l and w.
Count the number of squares that are cut by the diagonal.
Then check whether the formula gives the same answer.

   i $l = 7, w = 2$ **ii** $l = 10, w = 4$ **iii** $l = 8, w = 4$

10 This rectangle is 3 units wide and 4 units long.
It has 17 red dividers.

Arjun says that this formula gives the number
of dividers, d, needed by a rectangle of length l
and width w.

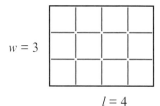

$w = 3$

$l = 4$

$d = (w - 1)l + (l - 1)w$

Divider ——

a   Does the formula work for this rectangle?

b   Check whether the formula works for the following rectangles.
Draw diagrams to show your working.

   i $l = 5, w = 3$ **ii** $l = 6, w = 2$ **iii** $l = 7, w = 1$

11 a   The sum of the first n square numbers is S. Copy and complete the table.

n	1	2	3	4	5
S	1	$1 + 4 = 5$	$1 + 4 + 9$ $= \square$	$1 + 4 + 9 + 16$ $= \square$	$1 + 4 + 9 + 16 + 25$ $= \square$

b   Here are three possible formulae for S. Only one is correct.

Which is the correct formula? Show how you decided.

   i $S = 4n - 3$ **ii** $S = \dfrac{5n^2 - 7n + 4}{2}$ **iii** $S = \dfrac{n(n + 1)(2n + 1)}{6}$

12 Brian writes four consecutive multiples of 3.

He multiplies the largest and smallest numbers together.

He subtracts this from the product of the middle two numbers.

The difference is $D = 108 - 90 = 18$

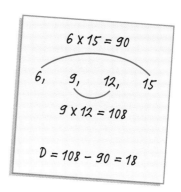

a Write another four consecutive multiples of 3 and find the difference D. Is the difference always 18?

b What is the difference, D, for four consecutive multiples of 2?

c Find the difference, D, for any four consecutive multiples of 4.

d What is D for any four consecutive multiples of 1?

e Copy and complete the table.
m represents the multiple and D the difference.

Multiple (m)	1	2	3	4	5	6
Difference (D)			18			

f Complete the formula. $D = 2 \times m^{\square}$

g Find D for these values of m.

i 7   **ii** 9   **iii** 10

13 Sally uses 12 red connectors to make a square of side length 2 units.

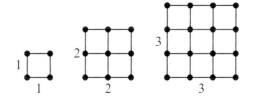

a Draw the next two squares. Copy and complete the table.

Side length of square (s)	1 unit	2 units	3 units	4 units	5 units
Number of connectors (c)	4	12			

b Copy and complete this formula. $c = \square\, s(s + 1)$

c Use your formula to find the number of connectors when $s = 8$.

d Sally has 200 connectors. What is the largest square she can make?

14 The diagram shows squares of side length 2 units and of side length 3 units.

To find T, multiply the numbers in opposite corners of the square, then add the products.

1	2
3	4

1	2	3
4	5	6
7	8	9

a Draw a similar square that has side length 4 units.

b For the square of side length 2 units, $T = (3 \times 2) + (1 \times 4) = 6 + 4 = 10$

For the square of side length 3 units, $T = (7 \times 3) + (1 \times 9) = 21 + 9 = 30$

Find T for the square of side length 4 units.

c n is the side length of a square. Check whether $T = n^3 + n$ is the correct formula for T by finding the value of T when $n = 2, 3,$ and 4.

15 This is the formula for the area of a triangle.

$\text{Area} = \frac{1}{2} \times \text{base} \times \text{height}$

a Use the formula to find the areas of these triangles.

i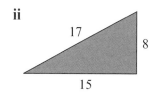

ii **iii**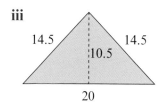

b The letters a, b, and c stand for the length of each side of a triangle.

$$s = \frac{a + b + c}{2} \qquad T = \sqrt{s(s - a)(s - b)(s - c)}$$

For each triangle in part **a**, find the values of s and T.

c What does the formula for T give?

16 Explain how to find the area of the triangle PQR.
Find the area of the triangle to the nearest square centimetre.

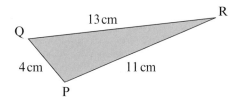

Use your answer to question **15c**.

Area

- Calculating the area of a triangle, parallelogram and trapezium
- Calculating the area of compound shapes
- Converting between measures of area such as mm^2 and cm^2

Keywords

You should know

explanation 1a | explanation 1b

1 Calculate the area of these triangles.

a

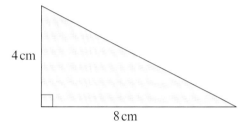

4 cm

8 cm

b

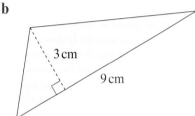

3 cm

9 cm

c

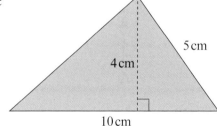

5 cm

4 cm

10 cm

d

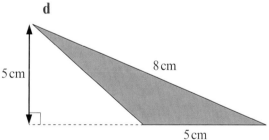

5 cm

8 cm

5 cm

2 Calculate the height of each triangle. (The area and the base length of each triangle is given.)

a Area = 25 cm^2

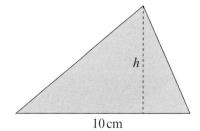

h

10 cm

b Area = 20 mm^2

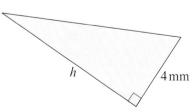

h

4 mm

3 Triangle B has double the area of triangle A.

The height of both triangles is 6 cm.

a Calculate the area of triangle A.

b What is the area of triangle B?

c Calculate the value of x.

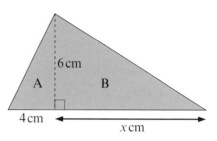

4 The area of triangle Y is three times that of triangle X.

a Calculate the area of triangle X.

b Calculate the area of triangle Y.

c Calculate the height of triangle Y.

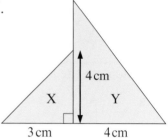

5 Look at this diagram.

a Calculate the area of triangle ABE.

b Calculate the area of triangle ACD.

c Calculate the area of the trapezium BCDE.

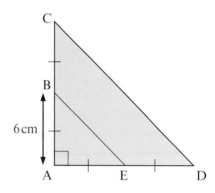

explanation 2a   explanation 2b

6 Calculate the area of these parallelograms.

a

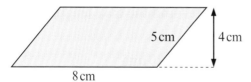

b

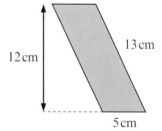

c

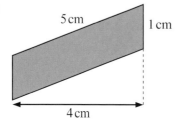

d

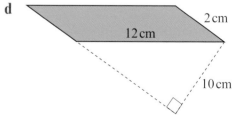

explanation 3a explanation 3b explanation 3c

7 Calculate the area of these trapeziums.

a

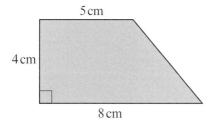

b

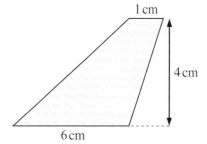

c

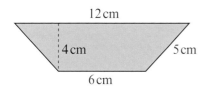

d

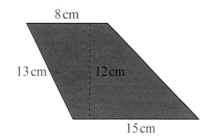

8 Calculate the marked lengths in these shapes.

a Area = $96 \, \text{cm}^2$

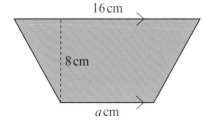

b Area = $51 \, \text{cm}^2$

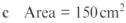

c Area = $150 \, \text{cm}^2$

d Area = $100 \, \text{cm}^2$

explanation 4

9 Calculate the area of these compound shapes.

a

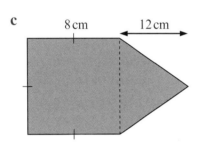

3 cm

8 cm

3 cm

20 cm

b

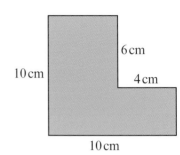

6 cm

10 cm

4 cm

10 cm

c

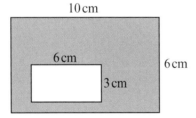

8 cm   12 cm

d

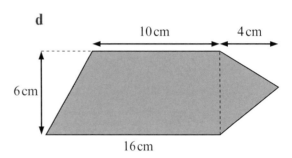

10 cm   4 cm

6 cm

16 cm

10 Calculate the shaded area of each of these.

a

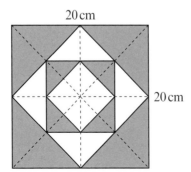

10 cm

6 cm

3 cm

6 cm

b

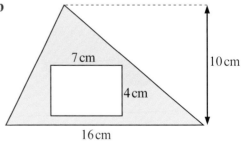

7 cm

4 cm

10 cm

16 cm

c

20 cm

20 cm

d

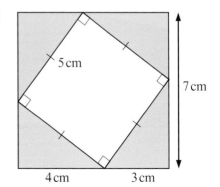

5 cm

7 cm

4 cm   3 cm

11 An arrowhead has dimensions as shown.

Showing your method clearly, calculate the shaded area.

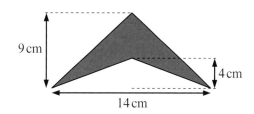

12 The side of a house has the dimensions shown. Showing your method clearly, calculate the area of this side of the house.

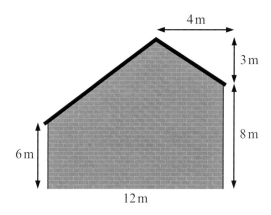

Hint: can you divide the shape into two trapeziums?

13 **a** Calculate the area that is shaded when x has these values.

    i $x = 6$

    ii $x = 8$

  b What do you notice about your answers to part **a**? Explain why this is.

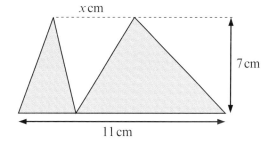

  c A piece of guttering has a cross-section as shown.

Calculate the area of the cross-section.

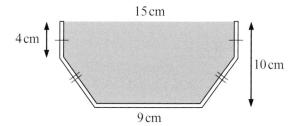

14 A garden consists of a rectangular
patch of grass, C, and two triangular
flowerbeds, A and B.

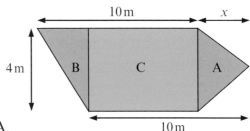

a Write an expression for the area of A.

b Write an expression for the area of B.

c Write an expression for the area of C.

d Work out the total area of the garden.

explanation 5

15 Measure a page of your exercise book.

a What is its area in square centimetres?

b What is its area in square millimetres?

16 Convert these areas to square millimetres.

a $15\,cm^2$ b $2.5\,cm^2$ c $580\,cm^2$ d $0.038\,cm^2$

17 Convert these areas to square centimetres.

a $25\,000\,mm^2$ b $6700\,mm^2$ c $37\,mm^2$ d $456.78\,mm^2$

18 A standard A6 postcard is 147 mm by 105 mm.

a What is its area in square millimetres?

b What is its area in square centimetres?

c A 1st class stamp (2.0 cm wide and 2.4 cm high) is stuck on the postcard.
What percentage of the area of the postcard does it cover?

19 Put these areas in order of size, smallest first.

$0.017\,m^2$ $2.61\,cm^2$ $72\,mm^2$ $582\,mm^2$ $68.4\,cm^2$

20 An A0 sheet of paper has an area of $1\,m^2$.

a What is its area in square centimetres?

b What is its area in square millimetres?

Volume

- Calculating the volume of cuboids and of shapes made of cuboids
- Calculating the surface area of cuboids and of shapes made of cuboids
- Calculating the surface area and volume of prisms
- Converting between measures of volume such as mm^3 and cm^3

Keywords

You should know

explanation 1a   explanation 1b   explanation 1c   explanation 1d

1 Calculate the volume of these cuboids.

a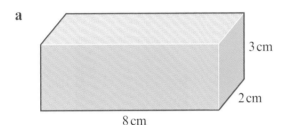

b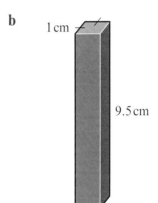

c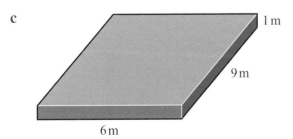

d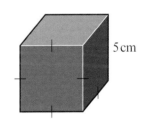

2 Calculate the total surface area of each cuboid in question **1**.

3 The volumes of these cuboids are given.

Calculate the lengths of the sides marked by letters.

a Volume = 96 cm^3

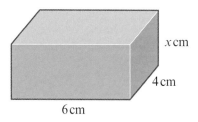

b Volume = 128 cm^3

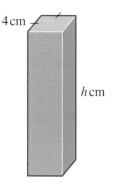

c Volume = 100 cm^3

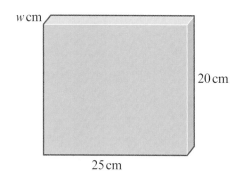

d Volume = 343 cm^3

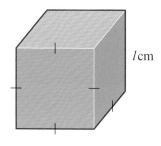

4 Calculate the total surface area of each of the cuboids in question **3**.

5 Two cuboids are stuck together to make this shape.

a Calculate the volume of the shape.

b What is the area of face A?

c Calculate the surface area of faces B, C, D and E.

d What is the total surface area of the shape?

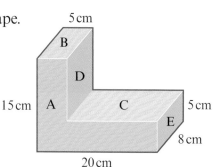

6 Two cuboids are stuck together to make this shape.

   a Calculate the volume of the shape.

   b Calculate the total surface area.

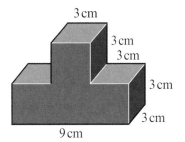

7 Three cuboids are stuck together to make this shape.

   a Calculate the volume of the shape.

   b Calculate the total surface area.

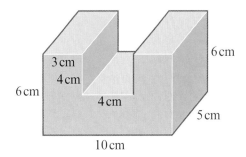

8 A cube of edge length 2 cm is placed on top of a cuboid.

   a What is the volume of the combined shape?

   b Calculate the total surface area of the shape.

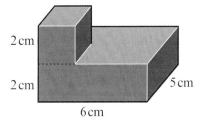

9 Cube A has edge length 2 cm.
The edges of cube B are twice as long as those of cube A.

   a Calculate the volume of cube A.

   b What is the total surface area of cube A?

   c How many times bigger is the volume of B compared to the volume of A?

   d How many times bigger is the surface area of B compared to the surface area of A?

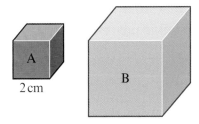

explanation 2

10 Work out the volume and surface area of each prism.

a

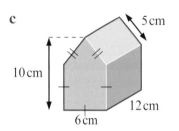

13 cm
12 cm
80 cm
10 cm

b

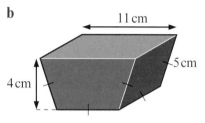

11 cm
5 cm
4 cm

c

5 cm
10 cm
12 cm
6 cm

d

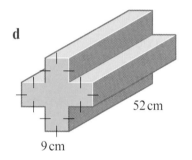

52 cm
9 cm

explanation 3

11 Measure the size of your textbook.

  a What is its volume in cubic centimetres (cm^3)?

  b What is its volume in cubic millimetres (mm^3)?

12 Convert these volumes to cubic millimetres.

  a $15\,cm^3$ **b** $2.5\,cm^3$ **c** $580\,cm^3$ **d** $0.038\,cm^3$

13 Convert these volumes to cubic centimetres.

  a $25\,000\,mm^3$ **b** $6700\,mm^3$ **c** $37\,mm^3$ **d** $456.78\,mm^3$

14 1 cubic metre $= 1\,m^3 = 1\,000\,000\,cm^3$

  a Estimate the volume of your classroom in cubic metres.

  b Convert your answer to cubic centimetres.

  c How many cubic millimetres is this?

  d A Multilink cube has a side of 2 cm. How many of these cubes could you fit into your classroom?

Plans and elevations

- Drawing plans and elevations of 3–D shapes
- Identifying nets of cubes and cuboids

Keywords

You should know

explanation 1

1 Which of these 3-D shapes are prisms?

> A prism has the same cross-section at any point along its length.

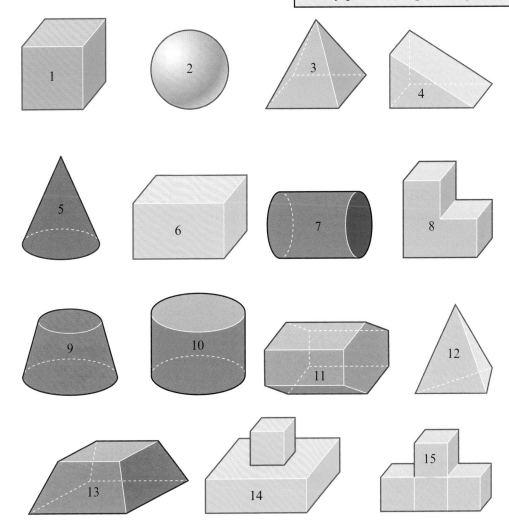

2 Which of the 3-D shapes in question **1** match to each plan below?

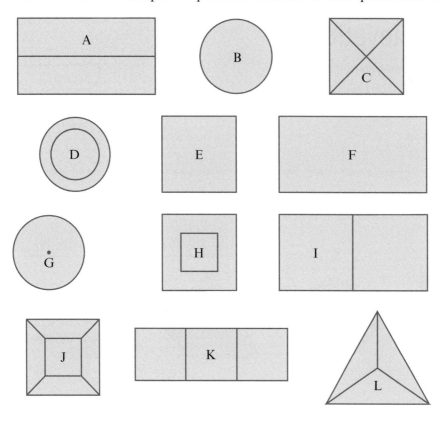

3 Which of the 3-D shapes for question **1** match to each side elevation below? Each elelvation shows the shape as seen from the right.

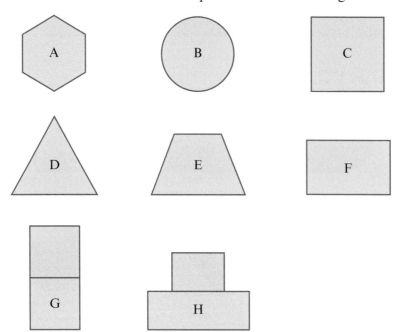

4 Each diagram shows a 3-D shape made from cubes.

  i Draw a plan of each shape.

  ii Draw a side elevation of each shape, as seen from the left.

a  **b** 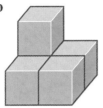 **c** 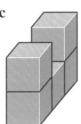 **d**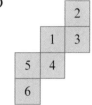

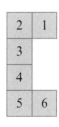

(explanation 2a) (explanation 2b) (explanation 2c)

5 a Which of these are nets of a cube?

A

	1	
2	3	4
	5	
	6	

B

3	2	1
4		
5		
6		

C

2	1
3	
4	
5	6

D

		2
	1	3
5	4	
6		

E

5			
4	1	2	3
6			

F

1			
2	3	4	5
			6

G

	5		
1	2	3	4
		6	

  b Look at your answers to part **a**. Imagine that each of those nets is folded to make a cube. For each net, which face would be opposite face 1 when folded?

6 There are 11 possible nets of a cube.

  a How many can you find? Draw them.

  b Which of the nets will tessellate?

> If shapes tessellate, they fit together like tiles to form a repeating pattern with no gaps.

  c Draw a diagram to show how one of the nets tessellates.

7 Draw two nets for this cuboid.

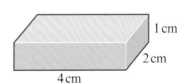

1 cm

2 cm

4 cm

Units of measurement

- Converting between metric units of length, area, volume and mass
- Justifying an appropriate degree of accuracy for a measurement
- Making rough conversions between metric and imperial measures

Keywords

You should know

explanation 1a   explanation 1b   explanation 1c

1 Copy and complete each statement.

a 8 km = ☐ m   **b** 1500 m = ☐ km   **c** 8.5 m = ☐ cm

d 70 cm = ☐ mm   **e** 0.65 m = ☐ mm   **f** 560 cm = ☐ km

g 2 hectares = ☐ m^2 **h** 5400 cm^2 = ☐ m^2 **i** 875 g = ☐ kg

j 1.305 kg = ☐ g   **k** 3.5 litres = ☐ cm^3 **l** 950 litres = ☐ m^3

2 Copy and complete the table. Choose from the items shown.
One has been done for you. Some items might not be used.

	Approximate measure	Type of measure	Item
	2 m	length	door
a	1 tonne		
b	750 ml		
c	7500 m^2		
d	100 g		
e	10 m		
f	480 mm^2		
g	200 litres		
h	1 kg		
i	50 cm^2		
j	15 cm		

3 On average, a person lives for about 40 000 000 minutes.

    a Giving your answers to one decimal place, work out how long this is in

       i hours

       ii days

      iii years

> In part **a iii**, assume that every year has 365 days.

    b How many leap years are there in an average lifetime?
      Give your answer to the nearest whole number.

> Hint: about one in every four years is a leap year. 'One in four' is the same as one quarter.

    c Taking leap years into account, convert your answer to part **a iii** into minutes.

      Is your answer longer or shorter than 40 000 000 minutes?

      Explain whether you think the difference is significant.

4 A fish tank is in the shape of a cuboid.
It can hold a maximum of 27 litres.
The base of the tank is made of plastic.
It is 25 cm wide and 50 cm long.

    a What is the height of the fish tank?

    b What is the area of glass needed to make the four sides of the tank?

5 Anthony is writing to his pen pal who lives in Paris.

    a Anthony says that the distance from Manchester to Paris is 600 km.
      What do you think this measurement is correct to?

      i To the nearest 10 metres   **ii** To the nearest 100 metres

     iii To the nearest kilometre   **iv** To the nearest 10 kilometres

    b Anthony says that the flight from Manchester to Paris takes 1.5 hours.
      What do you think this measurement is correct to?

      i To the nearest second   **ii** To the nearest 10 seconds

     iii To the nearest minute   **iv** To the nearest 10 minutes

      v To the nearest hour

explanation 2a   explanation 2b   explanation 2c

6   Approximately how many gallons will
these fuel tanks hold?
Give your answers to the nearest gallon.

a   55 litres

b   75 litres

c   80 litres

7 a   Convert these amounts to pounds. Write your answers to the nearest 0.1 lb.

i 1 kg   **ii** 1.5 kg   **iii** 500 g

b   Convert these amounts to kilograms. Write your answers to the nearest 0.1 kg.

i 2 lb   **ii** $5\frac{1}{2}$ lb

c   Sharon is going shopping. This is her shopping list.

Work out how much each item would cost to the
nearest penny at

i Greene's Grocers   **ii** Mason's Fruit & Veg

d   Sharon wants to do all her shopping at one shop.

Which shop should she choose if she wants to pay as little as possible?

1 kg bananas
2 lb mushrooms
500 g grapes
1.5 kg apples
$5\frac{1}{2}$ lb potatoes

8   In an athletics competition, Rosa runs in both the mile and the 1500 metres
races. Which race is longer and by how far?
Give your answer to the nearest 10 metres.

Functions

- Identifying a linear function
- Writing a function machine, using algebra
- Identifying and writing rules linking inputs and outputs
- Finding the inverse of a linear function

Keywords

You should know

explanation 1a   explanation 1b

1 Copy each function and find the outputs.

a input x output y

$-1, 0, 1, 2, 3 \rightarrow \boxed{+ 1} \rightarrow \boxed{\times 3} \rightarrow \Box, \Box, 6, \Box, \Box$

b $y = \dfrac{12}{x}$

Input (x)	1	2	3	4
Output (y)		6		

c $x \rightarrow \dfrac{x}{2} + 3$

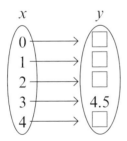

d $y = x^2 + 1$

Input (x)	1	2	3	4
Output (y)				17

4^2 is 4×4

So $4^2 + 1 = 17$

2 Which of the functions in question **1** are linear functions?
Give a reason for your answer.

3 Write each function machine as an equation.

a $x \rightarrow \boxed{\times 2} \rightarrow y$

b $x \rightarrow \boxed{+5} \rightarrow y$

c $x \rightarrow \boxed{-6} \rightarrow y$

d $x \rightarrow \boxed{\times 2} \rightarrow \boxed{+1} \rightarrow y$

e $q \rightarrow \boxed{\div 7} \rightarrow \boxed{-1} \rightarrow p$

f $t \rightarrow \boxed{+5} \rightarrow \boxed{\times 4} \rightarrow y$

g $b \rightarrow \boxed{-4} \rightarrow \boxed{\div 2} \rightarrow a$

h $k \rightarrow \boxed{\times 2} \rightarrow \boxed{\div 3} \rightarrow j$

(explanation 2a) (explanation 2b)

4 What is the rule that links each set of input and output numbers?
Write each rule as a function machine.

a

Input (x)	Output (y)
1	4
2	5
3	6
4	7
5	8

b

Input (x)	Output (y)
1	3
2	6
3	9
4	12
5	15

c

Input (x)	Output (y)
1	$\frac{1}{2}$
2	1
3	$1\frac{1}{2}$
4	2
5	$2\frac{1}{2}$

d

Input (x)	2	3	4	5	6
Output (y)	0	3	6	9	12

e

Input (x)	1	2	3	4	5
Output (y)	5	9	13	17	21

f

Input (x)	1	2	3	4	5
Output (y)	1.5	2	2.5	3	3.5

5 Write an equation for each of your function machines in question **4**.

explanation 3a   explanation 3b

6 Find the inverse of each function. Check that it does reverse the original function using a simple pair of input and output values.

a $x \rightarrow x + 3$

b $x \rightarrow x - 4$

c $x \rightarrow 10x$

d $x \rightarrow 7x + 1$

e $x \rightarrow 2x + 3$

f $x \rightarrow 4x - 3$

g $y = 2x - 15$

h $y = \frac{x}{4}$

i $y = \frac{x}{3} - 1$

j $y = \frac{x}{2} + 10$

k $x \rightarrow 2(x + 5)$

l $x \rightarrow 3(x - 1)$

m $x \rightarrow \frac{(x + 1)}{2}$

n $y = \frac{x - 3}{4}$

o $y = \frac{2x}{5}$

7 Find the function that links these inputs and outputs.

input x output y

$-1, 0, 1, 2, 3 \rightarrow$ ☐ → ☐ → $7, 9, 11, 13, 15$

8 Find the inverse of the function in question **7**. Check your answer.

9 Look at these inputs and outputs.

Input (x)	2	4	6	8	10
Output (y)	7	13	19	25	31

a What are the differences between the outputs?

b What would be the difference between the outputs if the input increased by 1 each time?

c Find the function that links the inputs and the outputs.

d Find the inverse function and check your answer.

10 This is the table of values for a linear function.

Input (x)	0	2	4	6	8	10	12
Output (y)	2			20			

a Copy and complete the table.

b What is the linear function?

c Find the inverse function and check your answer.

11 Lucy writes the function $y = 10 - 2x$.

    a Find the output when $x = 3$.

    b Lucy then writes the function as $y = -2x + 10$.

       Copy and complete the function machine.

$$x \rightarrow \boxed{\times \square} \rightarrow \boxed{+ \square} \rightarrow y$$

    c Find the inverse function.

    d Explain how you can check that your inverse function is correct.

12 Find the inverse of each function.

    Check that they do reverse the original functions.

    a $x \rightarrow 12 - 3x$ **b** $y = 8 - 2x$

    c $x \rightarrow 2 - x$ **d** $y = 6 - \dfrac{x}{2}$

13 Jim writes the function $y = 3 - 5x$.

    a **i** The output is the same as the input when the input value is a.
          Jim says that a is the solution of the equation $3 - 5a = a$.
          Explain why he is right. Solve the equation to find a.

       ii Find the inverse function. Check your answer.

    b Use your answers to part **a** to write down the solution of $3 - 5x = \dfrac{3 - x}{5}$.

       Explain how you know.

14 **a** Copy and complete the function machine for the function $y = \dfrac{9 - 2x}{7}$.

$$x \rightarrow \boxed{\times \square} \rightarrow \boxed{+ \square} \rightarrow \boxed{\div \square} \rightarrow y$$

    b Find the outputs when $x = 1$, 2 and 3. Explain whether this function is linear.

    c Write the inverse function.
       Check your answer using the output values you found in part **b**.

    d Use your answer to part **c** to solve these equations.

       i $\dfrac{9 - 2x}{7} = 8$ **ii** $\dfrac{9 - 2x}{7} = 1$

Functions and mappings

- Constructing a mapping diagram from a function machine
- Identifying a linear function

Keywords

You should know

explanation 1a   explanation 1b

1 Look at this pair of numbers.   5   and   −2

Work these out.

a   5 + −2   b   5 − −2

c   5 × −2   d   5 ÷ −2

2 Add, subtract, multiply and divide each of these pairs of numbers.

a   −6   −2   b   −4   − 8

c   9   −3   d   −10   +4

3 Copy and complete these function machines.

a

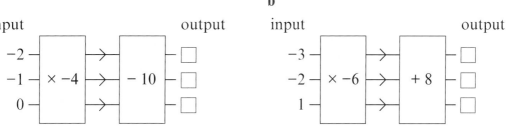

b

c

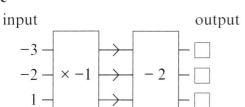

d

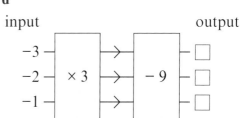

4 Find the output of each function when the input is −8.

    a $x \rightarrow 3x$ **b** $y = 15 - 2x$ **c** $x \rightarrow \dfrac{x}{2} - 1$ **d** $y = 5x + 4$

explanation 2a   explanation 2b

5 Look at this table of values for the function $x \rightarrow 4x + 1$.

Input (x)	−1	0	1	2	3
Output (y)					13

    a Copy and complete the table.

    b Explain why this is a linear function.

6 Look at this mapping diagram for $y = x + 2$.

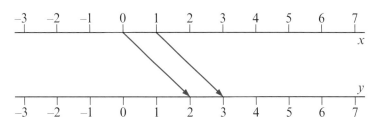

    a Copy and complete the mapping diagram.

    b Describe how the output changes as the inputs increase by 1.

    c Explain why this is a linear function.

7 $x \rightarrow 2x - 2$ is a mapping.

    a Write the mapping as a function machine.

    b Copy and complete the table and the mapping diagram.

Input (x)	Output (y)
−1	
0	
1	
2	2
3	
4	

    c Is the function a linear function? Explain your answer.

8 **a** Copy and complete the table for the function $x \rightarrow \frac{x}{2} + 3$.

Input (x)	0	1	2	3	4
Output (y)		3.5			

b Describe how the output is changing.

c Is this a linear function? Explain your answer.

9 $y = 4 - 2x$ is a mapping.

a Copy and complete the mapping diagram.

b Describe how the output changes.

c Explain why $y = 4 - 2x$ is a linear function.

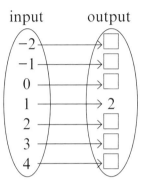

10 A linear function maps $2 \rightarrow 5$, as shown in the table.

Input (x)	−2	−1	0	1	2	3	4
Output (y)					5		

Write the linear function that also does the following mappings.
Copy and complete the table for each function.

a $1 \rightarrow 4$ **b** $1 \rightarrow 2$ **c** $3 \rightarrow 3$ **d** $0 \rightarrow 11$

explanation 3a   explanation 3b

11 **a** Which of these functions are linear? Explain how you know.

    i $x \rightarrow x(1 + x)$ **ii** $y = 3(x - 2)$

    iii $y = (x + 3)^3$ **iv** $x \rightarrow \frac{x + 1}{3}$

b **i** Write three different linear functions that map $1 \rightarrow 1$.

    ii For each function, write down the outputs when the input is 2, 3 and 4. Explain how the output pattern shows that the function is linear.

c **i** Write three different non-linear functions that map $1 \rightarrow 1$.

    ii For each function, write down the outputs when the input is 2, 3 and 4. Explain how the output pattern shows that the function is non-linear.

Functions and graphs

- Finding the gradient of the graph of a linear function
- Describing a straight line using an equation
- Recognising that straight lines can be written in the form $y = mx + c$
- Interpreting the equation of a line
- Drawing lines of linear functions in the form $ry + sx = t$

Keywords

You should know

explanation 1a   explanation 1b

1 Each line represents a linear function. Find the gradient of each line.

a

b
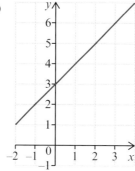

c
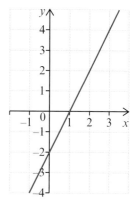

d
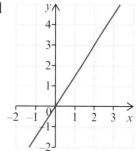

e
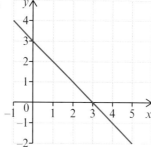

f
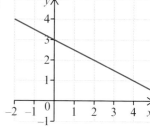

explanation 2

2 For each graph:

    i Write the coordinates of each point marked with a cross. Write your answers in a table.

x					
y					

    ii What is the gradient of the line?

    iii Write the equation of the line.

a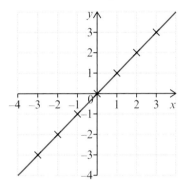

b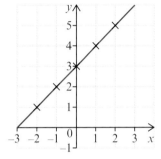

c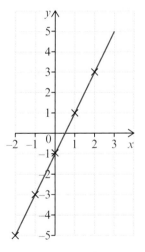

d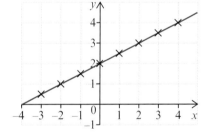

e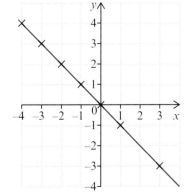

f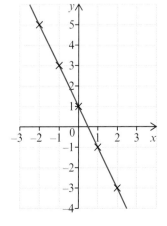

3 Charlotte draws a line that goes through (0, 1).

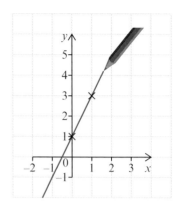

   a The gradient of the line is 2. Explain why the line must also go through (1, 3).

   b Write the equation of the line.

4 Steven draws a line through the point (0, 4).

   a The gradient of the line is −1. Explain why the line goes through (1, 3).

   b Write the equation of the line.

5 a Plot the points A (2, 1) and B (4, 0) on a copy of these axes.
Draw a straight line through both points.

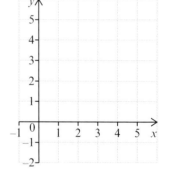

   b What is the gradient of the line?

   c Moving from A to B, the value of the input x increases by 2.
What is the change in the output y?

   d Find the change in y when x increases by

     i 1   **ii** 5   **iii** n

   e Describe a way to calculate the gradient of the line from the coordinates of points A and B.

   f Find the equation of the line.

6 Find the equation of the straight line passing through each pair of points.

   a (0, 0) and (1, 1)   **b** (0, 1) and (1, 3)   **c** (1, 2) and (3, 8)

   d (2, 0) and (−2, −2)   **e** (3, 1) and (7, 1)   **f** (−1, 2) and (−5, −10)

explanation 3a   explanation 3b

7 Find the equation of the red line and the blue line in each diagram.

a

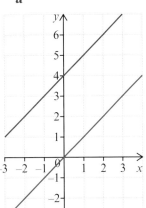

b

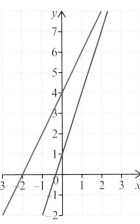

c

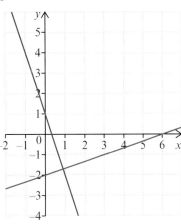

d

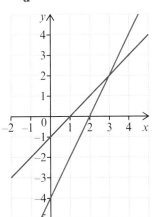

e

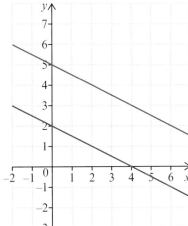

f

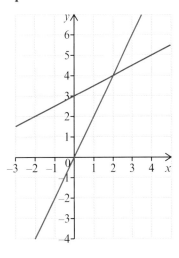

8 Look at your answers to question 7. What do parallel lines have in common?

9 Which of these lines is the steepest and which are parallel?

$y = 2 - x$ $y = x - 1$ $y = 2x - 1$ $y = 4x - 10$ $y = 2x$

explanation 4a   explanation 4b

10 Draw each pair of lines on a set of axes, where each goes from -5 to 8.
Write the coordinates of the point where they intersect.

a $y = 2x$, $y = 3 - x$ **b** $y = 3x - 2$, $y = 4$

c $y = x - 4$, $x = 4$ **d** $y + 2x = 4$, $y = x - 5$

e $2y + 3x = 6$, $y = -1.5$ **f** $2x + 7y = 14$, $y = 2$

g $x - 4y = 8$, $y = -1$ **h** $2y - 3x = 15$, $x = -3$

11 Draw these lines.

a $x + y = 0$ **b** $x - 2y = 0$ **c** $3x + 4y = 0$

12 Plot the graphs of $2x - 3y = 0$ and $x - 2y = 1$ on the same axes.
Write the coordinates of the point where the two lines meet.

13 **a** Draw the lines $y = 7x + 3$ and $4x + 3y + 1 = 0$ on the same axes.

b Estimate the coordinates of the point where the lines intersect.

c Explain why the x-coordinate of the point of intersection satisfies

$4x + 3(7x + 3) + 1 = 0$

d Solve the equation to find the exact coordinates of the point of
intersection.

14 Use a computer to plot these graphs or plot them yourself by completing a
simple table. Explain why only two are the graphs of linear functions.

a $y = x^2 - 4$ **b** $y = 2x - 4$

c $2x + y = 10$ **d** $y = \frac{4}{x}$

15 Use your graphs from question **14** to explain why two of these equations can
each have more than one solution. Which equations are they?

$x = x^2 - 4$ $x = 2x - 4$

$2x + x = 10$ $x = \frac{4}{x}$

> Look at the points of intersection
> between the graphs in question
> **14** and the line $y = x$. You do not
> need to solve the equations!

Place value, ordering and rounding

- Working with negative powers of 10
- Multiplying and dividing integers and decimals by any power of 10
- Rounding numbers to a given power of 10
- Rounding numbers to either 1 or 2 decimal places
- Rounding decimals to the nearest whole number

Keywords

You should know

explanation 1

1 Write these numbers as powers of 10.

   a one hundred   **b** one thousand   **c** ten

   d ten thousand   **e** one million   **f** one hundred thousand

   g one   **h** one billion

> One billion = one thousand million

2 Write these as powers of 10.

   a one hundredth   **b** one thousandth   **c** one millionth

3 Copy and complete these statements using powers of 10.

   a $1\,\text{m} = \square\,\text{cm}$ **b** $1\,\text{cm} = \square\,\text{m}$ **c** $1\,\text{cm} = \square\,\text{mm}$

   d $1\,\text{mm} = \square\,\text{cm}$ **e** $1\,\text{m} = \square\,\text{mm}$ **f** $1\,\text{mm} = \square\,\text{m}$

4 Tiny transistors inside computer chips are now as small as 45 nanometres.

One nanometre (nm) = one billionth of one metre.

Copy and complete each identity using a power of 10.

   a $1\,\text{nm} = \square\,\text{m}$ **b** $1\,\text{nm} = \square\,\text{mm}$ **c** $1\,\text{cm} = \square\,\text{nm}$

5 Write these expressions as numbers without using powers.

   a 2×10^2 **b** 4×10^3 **c** 9×10^4 **d** 7×10^5

   e 8×10^6 **f** 2.1×10^3 **g** 0.35×10^3 **h** 1.25×10^2

6 Write each number as a multiple of a power of 10.

   a   six hundred   **b**   five thousand   **c**   eighty thousand

   d   one hundred thousand   **e**   three million   **f**   two hundred million

   g   seven hundredths   **h**   nineteen thousandths

> **explanation 2a**   **explanation 2b**

7 Work these out without using a calculator.

   a 23×0.1 **b** 99×0.1 **c** 149×0.01

   d 8×0.01 **e** 765×0.001 **f** 55×0.001

   g 9×0.01 **h** $6581 \times 0.1 \times 0.01$ **i** $62 \times 0.01 \times 0.01$

8 Work these out without using a calculator.

   a $3 \div 0.1$ **b** $20 \div 0.1$ **c** $169 \div 0.1$

   d $100 \div 0.1$ **e** $2 \div 0.01$ **f** $14 \div 0.01$

   g $128 \div 0.01$ **h** $5 \div 0.1 \div 0.01$ **i** $85 \div 0.01 \div 0.01$

9 Find the missing numbers in each of these calculations.

   a $14 \times 0.1 = \square$ **b** $360 \times 0.01 = \square$ **c** $78 \times \square = 0.78$

   d $420 \times \square = 42$ **e** $\square \times 0.01 = 20$ **f** $\square \div 0.1 = 160$

   g $\square \div 0.01 = 3000$ **h** $35 \div \square = 350$ **i** $\square \div 0.01 = 27$

10 Copy and complete each diagram.

   a

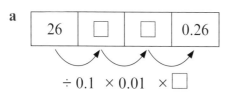

   b

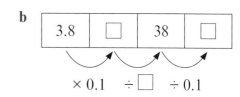

explanation 3

11 Write a multiplication and its answer for each diagram. The side length of each small square is $\frac{1}{10}$ of the side length of the large square.

a

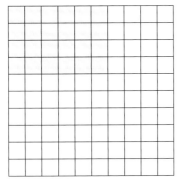

b

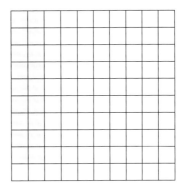

c

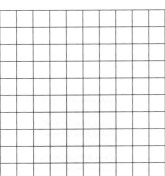

d

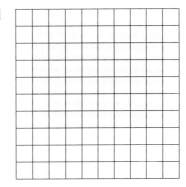

12 Write a division and its answer for each of the diagrams in question **11**.

13 Work these out without using a calculator.

   a 0.3×0.2 　　　 b 0.8×0.4 　　　 c 0.5×0.9

   d $0.6 \div 0.3$ 　　　 e $0.6 \div 0.2$ 　　　 f $0.9 \div 0.1$

14 Work these out without using a calculator.

   a 1.2×0.1 　　　 b 2.4×0.2 　　　 c 1.5×0.01

   d $2.5 \div 0.1$ 　　　 e $3.6 \div 0.01$ 　　　 f $4.8 \div 0.2$

15 Find the missing number in each calculation without using a calculator.

a $0.4 \times 0.1 = \square$

b $0.2 \times 0.01 = \square$

c $0.8 \times \square = 0.24$

d $0.7 \times \square = 0.56$

e $\square \times 0.01 = 0.03$

f $\square \times 0.01 = 0.006$

g $12 \times \square = 2.4$

h $\square \times 8 = 3.2$

> explanation 4

16 Round each number to the degree of accuracy given.

a 823 (nearest 100)

b 102 (nearest 10)

c 1678 (nearest 1000)

d 2590 (nearest 100)

e 500 (nearest 1000)

f 20 999 (nearest 1000)

17 a The number of people attending a football match is exactly 67 189.

Round the number to these degrees of accuracy.

i the nearest 10

ii the nearest 100

iii the nearest 1000

iv the nearest 10 000

b The number of people voting in a local election was recorded as exactly 1 628 599.

Round the number to these degrees of accuracy.

i the nearest million

ii the nearest 100 000

iii the nearest 10 000

iv the nearest 1000

v the nearest 100

vi the nearest 10

18 Round these measurements to the degree of accuracy given.

a 27 mm (nearest centimetre)

b 384 mm (nearest centimetre)

c 9721 ml (nearest litre)

d 448 cm (nearest metre)

e 17 600 g (nearest kilogram)

f 957 mm^2 (nearest square centimetre)

explanation 5a   explanation 5b

19 Round each number to 1 decimal place.

    a   23.69   **b**   1.82   **c**   9.94   **d**   6.97

    e   19.93   **f**   19.98   **g**   19.95   **h**   100.04

20 Round each number to 2 decimal places.

    a   41.671   **b**   80.0453   **c**   1.007   **d**   30.0045

    e   3.3333...   **f**   6.6666...   **g**   9.9999...   **h**   100.0045

21 Use a calculator to do each calculation.
Write your answer to the number of decimal places (d.p.) given.

    a $6 \div 9$ (1 d.p.)   **b** $17 \div 11$ (1 d.p.)   **c** $17 \div 11$ (2 d.p.)

    d $14 \div 17$ (1 d.p.)   **e** $20 \div 100$ (2 d.p.)   **f** $7 \div 9$ (2 d.p.)

22 Use a calculator to find the area of each shape.
Write your answer to the nearest whole number.

a

5.82 cm

12.65 cm

b

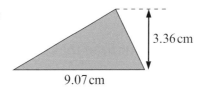

3.36 cm

9.07 cm

c

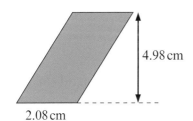

4.98 cm

2.08 cm

d

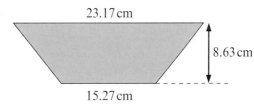

23.17 cm

8.63 cm

15.27 cm

23 A square has area 60 cm². Use a calculator to find these lengths.
Write your answers to the nearest centimetre.

    a   The length of each side of the square

    b   The perimeter of the square

Mental methods (2)

- Knowing mental strategies for working out calculations
- Knowing mental strategies for solving problems involving fractions, decimals and percentages
- Estimating the square roots of non-square numbers
- Estimating the answer to calculations by rounding

Keywords

You should know

explanation 1a   explanation 1b

1 Work out these sums mentally.

a 55 + 42	**b** 62 + 35	**c** 81 + 16	**d** 143 + 36
e 351 + 28	**f** 475 + 38	**g** 1726 + 77	**h** 2326 + 1685

2 Work out these subtractions mentally.

a 76 − 54	**b** 81 − 24	**c** 197 − 63	**d** 156 − 87
e 572 − 98	**f** 820 − 342	**g** 382 − 165	**h** 2460 − 159

3 Work out in your head the change given for each item of shopping.

a Seven pens costing 48p each and paid for using a £5.00 note.

b A rubber costing 37p and a ruler costing 54p paid for using a £1.00 coin.

c A magazine costing £1.70 and a newspaper costing 63p paid for using a £5.00 note.

d Some fruit costing £2.68 and some flowers costing £3.75 paid for using a £10.00 note.

e Food costing £38.72 and paid for using a £50.00 note.

f A service for a car costing £129.25 and paid for using three £50.00 notes.

explanation 2

4 Work out these multiplications mentally.

   a 27×0.2 **b** 55×0.3 **c** 72×0.4 **d** 125×0.02

   e 320×0.04 **f** 410×0.05 **g** 228×0.02 **h** 820×0.04

5 **a** A child's moneybox contains thirty-six 20p coins.
How much money, in pounds, is this?

   b A biro cost 40p. Calculate the cost, in pounds, of buying sixty biros.

   c A sausage machine produces one hundred and twenty sausages each hour.
Each sausage is 8 cm long.

     Calculate the total length, in metres, of sausages produced in these times.

     i 1 hour   **ii** 8 hours

   d A child's footprint is 15 cm long. Calculate the total distance, in metres, walked after two hundred and eighty footsteps when she walks so that her footsteps lie end to end.

explanation 3

6 Work out these multiplications mentally.

   a 23×11 **b** 16×11 **c** 32×12 **d** 45×19

   e 65×19 **f** 125×29 **g** 140×51 **h** 23×99

7 Work these out.

   a The total number of pupils in 22 classes of 31 pupils each.

   b The area of a rectangle 32 cm long and 19 cm wide.

   c The area of a square garden of edge length 29 m.

   d The number of chairs in a hall, when there are 29 rows and 15 chairs in each row.

8 Work these out mentally.

   a $220 + 6 \times 19$ **b** $39 \times 8 - 71 \times 3$ **c** 49^2

9 59 people pay £19.99 each to go on a coach trip.

Work out mentally how much they pay altogether.

explanation 4

10 Work these out mentally.

a 930 ÷ 15	**b** 612 ÷ 12	**c** 504 ÷ 18	**d** 288 ÷ 9
e 720 ÷ 120	**f** 1155 ÷ 21	**g** 784 ÷ 28	**h** 2688 ÷ 24
i 207 ÷ 1.8	**j** 155 ÷ 2.5	**k** 119 ÷ 0.35	**l** 22.56 ÷ 0.16

11 Work these out.

a 810 people are split equally into 15 groups.

How many people are there in each group?

b A lottery win of £115 680 is shared equally by a syndicate of 12 people.

How much does each person receive?

12 Rob can walk 2.6 miles in an hour. He is planning an 11.7 mile walk. Without using a calculator, work out how long it will take him to complete the walk.

explanation 5a explanation 5b explanation 5c

13 Copy and complete these tables without using a calculator.

Decimal	Fraction	Percentage
	$\frac{1}{2}$	
0.25		
0.333…		
	$\frac{1}{10}$	
		20%
0.666…		
	$\frac{3}{4}$	

Decimal	Fraction	Percentage
	$\frac{1}{8}$	
	$\frac{5}{8}$	
		80%
		150%
1.2		
	$\frac{29}{20}$	
	$\frac{5}{2}$	

14 Work these out mentally.

a   50% of 40   b   25% of 80   c $\frac{1}{10}$ of 120   d $\frac{3}{10}$ of 120

e   0.1 of 70   f   0.4 of 70   g   60% of 70   h $\frac{2}{3}$ of 93

i $\frac{1}{8}$ of 248   j $\frac{5}{8}$ of 248   k   120% of 50   l   160% of 90

m   240% of 60   n   175% of 100   o   2% of 110   p   105% of 6

15 Work these out without using a calculator.

a   In a school of 320 pupils 45% are girls. How many girls are there?

b   In a typical family, $\frac{3}{8}$ of income is spent on food. Calculate how much is spent on food by a family with a monthly income of £1200.

c   In a survey of 450 earthworms, it was found that 36% were over 6 cm in length. How many earthworms in the survey were over 6 cm long?

d   Due to high demand, a shop decides to increase the price of one of its games consoles by 11%.
If the original price was £180, calculate the new selling price.

e   Better Books decides to reduce the price of its books by $\frac{1}{3}$.
What is the new price of a book that was originally selling for £24.90?

129

explanation 6

16 Use estimation to match the value of each square root to a number in the box.

9.2	8.8	4.9
10.4	20.2	5.8
12.2	2.2	1.4

a $\sqrt{5}$ **b** $\sqrt{24}$ **c** $\sqrt{84}$

d $\sqrt{108}$ **e** $\sqrt{77}$ **f** $\sqrt{2}$

g $\sqrt{150}$ **h** $\sqrt{410}$ **i** $\sqrt{34}$

17 Use your answers to question **16** to help find the approximate length of the side of a square with each area.

a Area $= 34\,\text{cm}^2$ **b** Area $= 108\,\text{m}^2$ **c** Area $= 5\,\text{m}^2$

explanation 7a   explanation 7b

18 Estimate the answer to each calculation, showing your method clearly.

a 62×39 **b** 71×48 **c** 321×148

d $242 \div 62$ **e** $389 \div 47$ **f** $\dfrac{12 \times 31}{5}$

g $\dfrac{189 \times 211}{8}$ **h** $8 \times \sqrt{17}$ **i** $\sqrt{52} \times \sqrt{14}$

j $\dfrac{\sqrt{15} \times 89}{4}$ **k** $\dfrac{\sqrt{125} \times \sqrt{67}}{\sqrt{15}}$ **l** $23^2 \times \sqrt{6}$

m $\dfrac{31^2}{9 \times \sqrt{105}}$ **n** $19^2 \times 41^2 \times \sqrt{10}$ **o** $\left(\dfrac{1}{3}\right)^2 \times 385$

19 Sean estimates the value of $\dfrac{36 \times 29}{0.7}$ using $\dfrac{40 \times 30}{0.5}$.

a Find the value of Sean's estimate.
   Is this larger or smaller than the true value?

b Find a way to improve on Sean's estimate and work it out.

c Use a calculator to find the true value to the nearest whole number.

Written methods

- Written methods for adding, subtracting, multiplying and dividing decimals

Keywords

You should know

Unless stated otherwise, no calculators should be used in this topic.

explanation 1

1 Work out these additions.

a 25.1 + 13.6	**b** 126.2 + 31	**c** 826.4 + 3.9
d 431.8 + 9.25	**e** 34.9 + 3.06	**f** 459.7 + 28.36
g 69 + 837.26	**h** 0.38 + 640.9	**i** 0.279 + 12.83 + 59

2 Work these out.

a 42.2 + 3.4 + 18.2	**b** 12.9 + 8.3 + 18
c 102.37 + 19.62 + 0.04	**d** 1312 + 106.04 + 13.1
e 1406.7 + 19.38 + 1.063	**f** 26.9 + 0.1 + 127.329 + 3.88

explanation 2a explanation 2b

3 Work out these subtractions.

a 48.3 − 26.1	**b** 98.7 − 13.7	**c** 68.2 − 46.3
d 142.8 − 17.4	**e** 826.5 − 7.9	**f** 312.4 − 286.7
g 319.07 − 4.4	**h** 382.06 − 291.77	**i** 6 − 0.5732

4 Work these out.

a 412.98 − 12.3 − 2.04	**b** 308.64 − 14.11 − 19.01
c 901.3 − 312.4 − 27.01	**d** 38.7 + 123.9 − 3.04
e 67.4 + 33.12 − 91.3 + 48.04	**f** 104 − 3.06 + 72.7 − 81.926

5 a The heights of three pupils are 1.80 m, 1.76 m and 1.69 m.

   Calculate the combined height of the three pupils.

b Four apples have masses of 0.15 kg, 0.136 kg, 0.098 kg and 0.127 kg.

   Calculate their total mass.

c A car is parked in a garage with dimensions as shown.

   Calculate the value of x.

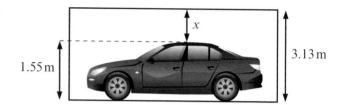

d A cave is 4.62 m tall. A stalactite growing down from the ceiling is 1.38 m long, whilst a stalagmite directly below it, is 0.87 m tall.

   Calculate the distance, d, between them.

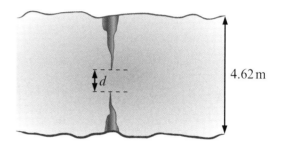

e Three crates A, B and C are arranged in the back of a lorry 3.68 m long as shown.

   Crate A is 0.2 m long, crate B is 0.86 m long and crate C is 1.05 m long.

   Calculate the remaining length, l.

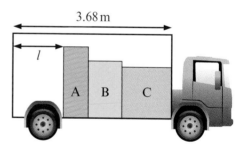

f Three packets X, Y and Z are weighed at the post office. Their combined mass is 12.63 kg.

   Y has a mass of 2.2 kg and Z has a mass of 6.49 kg.

   Calculate the mass of packet X.

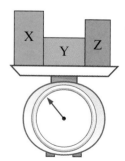

explanation 3a   explanation 3b

6 For each calculation

    i estimate the answer

    ii without a calculator, work out the answer

  a 32×2.5 **b** 820×4.1 **c** 98×4.7

  d 125×3.62 **e** 178×12.4 **f** 168×14.6

  g 24.4×6.8 **h** 34.4×28.3 **i** 126.1×2.04

7 a 56.4 g of cake mix is used to make a small cake.
How much cake mix is used to make 62 cakes?

  b The cost of a pencil is £0.18, calculate the cost of buying 86 pencils.

  c A magazine costs £2.42 per month.
Calculate the cost of a year's subscription.

  d A rectangular garden is 23.4 m long and 8.7 m wide. Calculate its area.

explanation 4a   explanation 4b   explanation 4c

8 Work these out.

  a $92.8 \div 16$ **b** $178.2 \div 22$ **c** $223.2 \div 24$

  d $225.6 \div 48$ **e** $38.72 \div 32$ **f** $5.661 \div 37$

9 Write down a three-digit number then write it down again to make a six-digit number.
Divide the six-digit number by 7,
then by 11 and then by 13.
What do you notice about your answer?
Explain why this happens.

> Working out $7 \times 11 \times 13$ might help you.

10 Work out the answers to the following divisions.

  a $32 \div 0.8$ **b** $3.64 \div 0.7$ **c** $153 \div 0.6$

  d $0.345 \div 0.05$ **e** $31.14 \div 0.9$ **f** $0.739 \div 0.02$

  g $531 \div 0.03$ **h** $0.741 \div 0.05$ **i** $4.36 \div 0.08$

  j $63.9 \div 1.5$ **k** $0.245 \div 0.14$ **l** $268.38 \div 6.3$

11 The area of each shape is given. Calculate the unknown lengths.

a
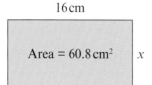

b
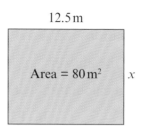

c
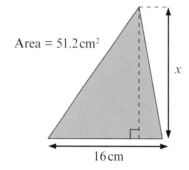

d
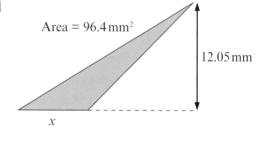

12 Use division to write these fractions as decimals.

a $\dfrac{5}{16}$ **b** $\dfrac{11}{16}$ **c** $\dfrac{9}{25}$

d $\dfrac{7}{8}$ **e** $\dfrac{17}{40}$ **f** $\dfrac{21}{32}$

13 Write these in order of size, smallest first. Show your method.

a 58%, $\dfrac{23}{40}$, $\dfrac{9}{16}$, 0.57   **b** 0.31, $\dfrac{8}{25}$, $\dfrac{9}{32}$, 30.7%

14 Find the value of x to make these scales balance.

a
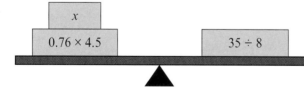

b

Using a calculator

- Using a calculator for more complex calculations
- Writing answers using a format consistent with the question
- Converting time given in decimal format into hours, minutes and seconds
- Using unrounded numbers in calculations that rely on previous results

explanation 1a   explanation 1b

1 For each calculation

   i work out the answer using a calculator

   ii check your answer by doing the calculation in your head

a $\dfrac{6+4}{2}$ **b** $\dfrac{6}{2}+4$ **c** $6+\dfrac{4}{2}$ **d** $\dfrac{20-8}{4}$

e $\dfrac{20}{4}-8$ **f** $20-\dfrac{8}{4}$ **g** $\dfrac{5^2+15}{10}$ **h** $\dfrac{5^2}{10}+15$

i $5^2+\dfrac{15}{10}$ **j** $\dfrac{(12-8)^2}{2}$ **k** $\dfrac{12^2-8^2}{2}$ **l** $\dfrac{12^2}{2}-\dfrac{8^2}{2}$

2 Use a calculator to work these out.

a $\dfrac{3.6+2.1^2}{6-5.1}$ **b** $\dfrac{22^2-3.8^2}{17+8}$ **c** $\dfrac{48-(3.7+9.8)^2}{5}$

d $4.1\times(8.6-2.5)^2$ **e** $(3.2\times6.8)^2-(8.1\times2.1)^2$ **f** $\left(\dfrac{3.8}{19}\right)^2-3.6$

g $\dfrac{8.5}{10\times3.4}+6.2$ **h** $\sqrt{\dfrac{4.5\times8}{4}}$ **i** $\sqrt{\dfrac{28\times3}{4.2\times5}}+9$

3 The formula for converting degrees Celsius (°C) to degrees Fahrenheit (°F) is $F=\dfrac{9}{5}C+32$

a Use a calculator to convert these temperatures from °C to °F.

   i 30°C   **ii** 18°C   **iii** 0°C   **iv** −5°C   **v** −40°C

b In order to estimate each answer, the formula can be rewritten as $F\approx 2C+30$.

   Without a calculator, estimate the answers to part **a** using this formula.

4 a   Copy and complete this function machine for the formula $F = \frac{9}{5}C + 32$

$C \rightarrow$ ▢ $\rightarrow$ ▢ $\rightarrow$ ▢ $\rightarrow F$

b   Draw the inverse function machine and use it to write a formula for converting degrees Fahrenheit (°F) to degrees Celsius (°C).

c   Use a calculator to convert these temperatures from °F to °C.

    i   100 °F   **ii**   70 °F   **iii**   0 °F

    iv   32 °F   **v**   −40 °F   **vi**   −76 °F

d   In order to estimate each answer, the formula can be rewritten as

$$C \approx \frac{1}{2}F - 15$$

Without a calculator, estimate the answers to part **c** using this formula.

(explanation 2a) (explanation 2b)

Use the following information to answer questions **5–8**.
These were the exchange rates between pounds (£)
and some other currencies in December 2007.

        £1 = 1.41 euros
        £1 = 228.49 Japanese yen
        £1 = 2.06 US dollars
        £1 = 15.21 Chinese yuan

5   Assuming there are no additional bank charges, calculate the amount in pounds that would be given in exchange for these amounts.

    a   1000 euros   **b**   500 US dollars

    c   10 000 Japanese yen   **d**   600 Chinese yuan

    e   400 euros and 8000 Japanese yen

    f   450 US dollars, 320 Chinese yuan and 6500 Japanese yen

6 **a** How many US dollars are equivalent to 500 euros?

    b How many Chinese yuan are equivalent to 650 Japanese yen?

    c How many euros are equivalent to 100 Japanese yen?

    d How many US dollars are equivalent to 10.20 Chinese yuan?

7 **a** A family of four, pay $67 for a meal while on holiday in the USA. Calculate the cost of the meal in pounds.

    b A couple pay 650 yuan for an extra tour whilst visiting China. Calculate the price of the tour in pounds.

    c An American on holiday in Europe pays 86 euros for a train journey. Calculate the cost of the train ticket in US dollars.

8 **a** Work out the new exchange rate for euros, US dollars, yen and yuan if the value of the pound increases by 15% from its value in December 2007.

    b Work out the new exchange rate for euros, US dollars, yen and yuan if the value of the pound decreases by 7% from its value in December 2007.

9 Mark went to Italy on holiday in December 2007.
He changed £150 into euros.

He went on holiday the following year and again changed £150 into euros, but during the year the value of the pound had fallen against the euro by 9%.

How many fewer euros did Mark get on his second holiday?

> explanation 3

10 Write each of these parts of a day in hours.

    a 0.5 of a day   **b** 0.75 of a day   **c** 0.625 of a day

11 Write each of these parts of an hour in minutes.

    a 0.2 of an hour   **b** 0.75 of an hour   **c** $0.8\dot{3}$ of an hour

    d $0.\dot{6}$ of an hour   **e** 0.35 of an hour   **f** $0.3\dot{6}$ of an hour

12 Write these times in hours and minutes.

    a 3.5 hours   **b** 4.75 hours   **c** 1.8 hours

    d 1.1 hours   **e** 7.65 hours   **f** 12.35 hours

13 A pupil spends $\frac{1}{3}$ of the day sleeping and $\frac{1}{10}$ of the day eating.

    a Calculate the total amount of time he spends either eating or sleeping.

        Give your answer in hours and minutes.

    b He spends $\frac{1}{4}$ of the remaining time playing with friends.

        How many hours and minutes is this?

14 Over a period of 5 hours in an evening Sage spent $\frac{1}{4}$ of the time doing her homework, $\frac{1}{3}$ of the time watching television, $\frac{1}{8}$ of the time talking to friends on the phone and the rest of the time doing other things.

    Calculate the following.

    a The time in hours and minutes that she spent doing homework.

    b The time in hours and minutes that she spent watching television.

    c The time in hours and minutes that she spent talking to friends.

    d The fraction of her evening spent doing other things.

    e The time in hours and minutes that she spent doing other things.

15 The Earth takes approximately 365 days (1 year) to orbit the Sun. It therefore takes 365 days to do a full 360° rotation around the Sun.

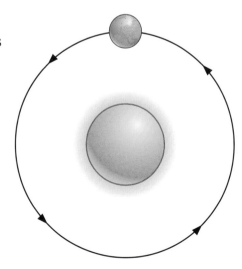

    Calculate the number of days, hours and minutes it takes to rotate the following number of degrees around the Sun.

    a 180°   **b** 90°   **c** 10°

    d 1°   **e** 17°

16 The Earth takes 24 hours (1 day) to rotate 360° on its axis.
Calculate the number of hours and minutes the Earth takes to rotate through the following angles.

   a 60°   **b** 45°   **c** 20°   **d** 1°   **e** 19°

> explanation 4

17 $p = \sqrt{5}$ and $q = \dfrac{74}{p - 2}$

   a Calculate the value of p to 1 d.p.

   b Calculate the value of q to 1 d.p.

   c Zac tries to calculate q using the rounded value of p. What is Zac's answer?

> Remember to use the **Ans** key.

18 A stack of 9 tiles has a height of 110 mm.

   a Calculate the thickness of each tile to the nearest millimetre.

   b How many of these tiles will fit under a shelf 300 mm high?

19 The area of a square is $8 \, \text{cm}^2$.

   a Calculate the length of each side of the square to the nearest centimetre.

   b Calculate the perimeter of the square to the nearest centimetre.

20 The volume of a cube is $160 \, \text{cm}^3$.

   a Calculate the length of each edge of the cube to the nearest centimetre.

   b Calculate the area of each face of the cube to the nearest square centimetre.

21 A tourist was given the exchange rate 248 Mexican pesos for £12.153 243 8.

   a What was the value of £1 to the nearest Mexican peso?

   b What was the value of £735 to the nearest Mexican peso?

Congruence

● Identifying congruent shapes, including triangles and quadrilaterals

Keywords

You should know

explanation 1

1 Draw a square like this on squared paper.

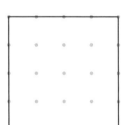

a Split the square into two congruent shapes. Each line you draw must start and end on a dot and be parallel to a side of the square.

b What is the smallest perimeter each of the congruent shapes can have? What is the largest perimeter? Draw diagrams to support your answer.

2 On squared paper, draw a square like the one in question **1**.

a Split the square into four congruent shapes. Each line you draw must start and end on a dot and be parallel to a side of the square.

b What is the smallest perimeter each of the congruent shapes can have? What is the largest perimeter? Draw diagrams to support your answer.

3 Draw an equilateral triangle on isometric paper.

a Split the triangle into three congruent shapes. Each line you draw must start and end on a dot and be parallel to a side of the triangle.

b What is the smallest perimeter each of the congruent shapes can have? What is the largest perimeter? Draw diagrams to support your answer.

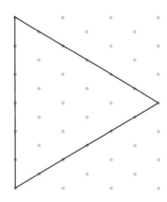

4 Which of these shapes are congruent to shape X?

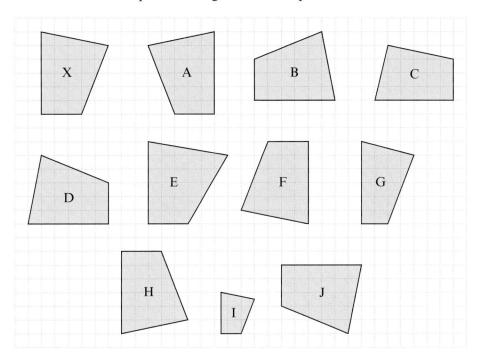

explanation 2

5 Which of the following triangles are definitely congruent to each other? Explain your answers.

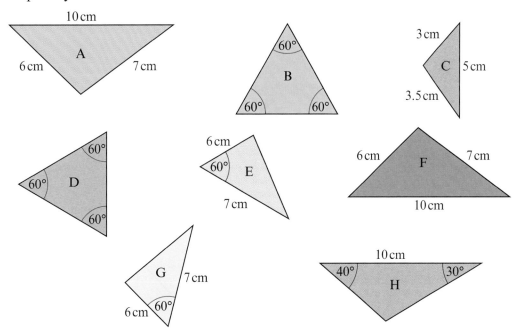

Reflection, rotation and translation

- Knowing that translations, rotations and reflections preserve length and angle and map on to congruent images
- Carrying out combinations of reflections, rotations and translations
- Finding the symmetry properties of two-dimensional shapes
- Identifying and sketching planes of symmetry of 3-D solids

Keywords

You should know

explanation 1a   explanation 1b   explanation 1c

1 Copy each diagram. Reflect each shape in the line $x = 2$.

a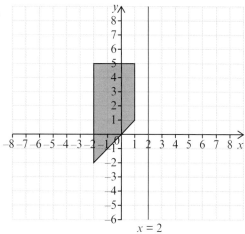

b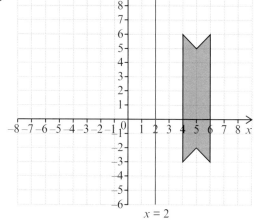

2 Copy each diagram. Reflect each shape in the line $y = x$.

a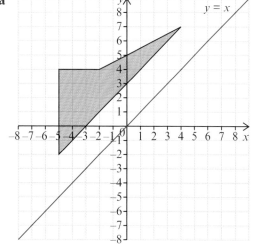

b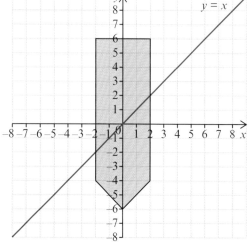

explanation 2a   explanation 2b

3 Copy each diagram. Rotate each shape 180° about (0, 0).

a
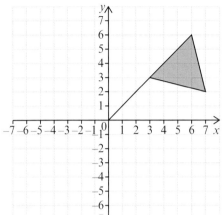

b
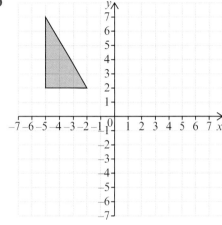

4 Copy each diagram. Rotate each shape 90° anticlockwise about the point shown.

a
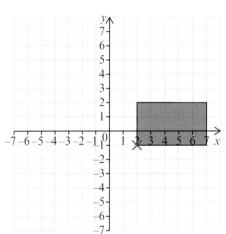

b
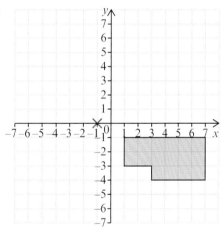

5 In each diagram, shape B is the image of object A after a single rotation.
Describe each rotation fully.

a
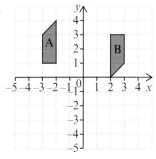

b
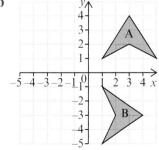

explanation 3a   explanation 3b

6 Copy each diagram. Translate each shape by the translation given.

a Translation $\begin{pmatrix} 5 \\ -8 \end{pmatrix}$

b Translation $\begin{pmatrix} -4 \\ -7 \end{pmatrix}$

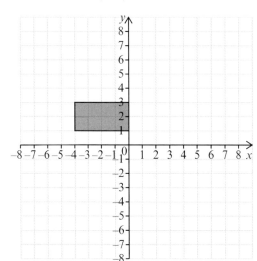
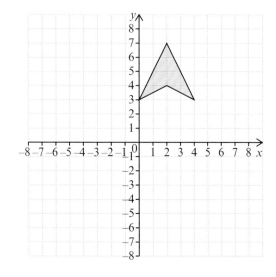

7 a X has been translated to each of the shapes A, B, C and D. Describe the translation that has taken place each time. The first one has been done for you.

X to A: translation $\begin{pmatrix} 4 \\ 2 \end{pmatrix}$

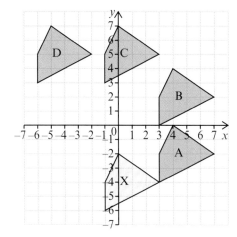

b Describe the translation A to B. Explain how you could work out this translation from your answers to part **a**, without using a diagram.

explanation 4a   explanation 4b

8 Copy each diagram. Reflect each shape in the *x*-axis and then reflect each image in the *y*-axis.

a

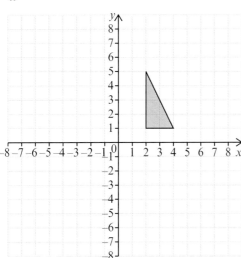

b

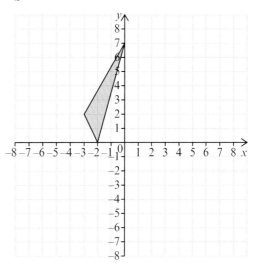

c

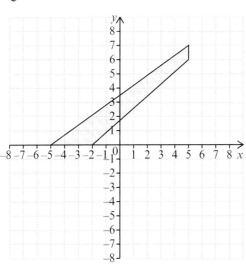

d

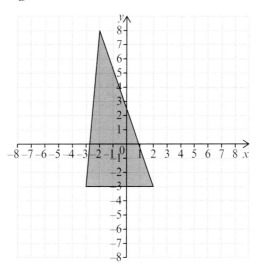

9 Look at your answers to question **8**.
What is the equivalent transformation for each combination of reflections?

10 Copy the diagrams in question **8**.
Reflect each shape in the *y*-axis and then reflect each image in the *x*-axis.

11 Look at your answers to question **10**.
What is the equivalent transformation for each combination of reflections?

12 Copy each diagram.

   a **i** Reflect the shape in the line
$x = 1$ and then reflect the
image in the line $y = -2$.

      ii What is the equivalent
single transformation?

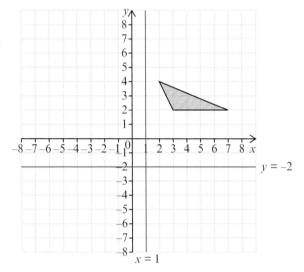

   b **i** Reflect the shape in the line
$y = 3$ and then reflect the
image in the line $x = 3$.

      ii What is the equivalent
single transformation?

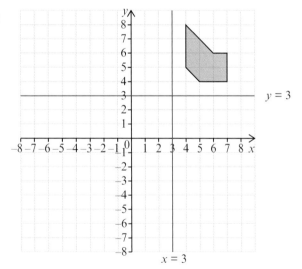

13 Copy this diagram onto squared paper.

a Reflect shape ABC in the mirror line M$_1$. Label the image A'B'C'.

b Reflect image A'B'C' in the mirror line M$_2$. Label this image A"B"C".

c What do you notice about the lengths AA" and M$_1$M$_2$?

d What single transformation is equivalent to the two reflections?

14 Copy these diagrams. Draw the image of each shape after it has undergone the set of transformations given. Mark the image of point A and label it A'.

a Reflection in the y-axis and then translation $\begin{pmatrix} -4 \\ -2 \end{pmatrix}$.

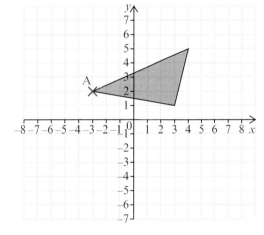

b Rotation 90° clockwise, centre (0, 0), and then translation $\begin{pmatrix} 5 \\ 3 \end{pmatrix}$.

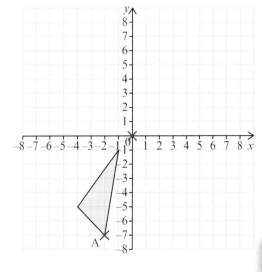

147

15 Repeat question **14**, but this time carry out the transformations in the reverse order. What do you notice about your answers compared to your answer to question **14**?

16 a Copy the diagram. Draw the image of the shape after the following set of three transformations. Mark the image of point A and label it A'.

Rotation 180° with centre (1, 0), then reflection in the *x*-axis, and then translation $\begin{pmatrix} -4 \\ -4 \end{pmatrix}$.

b Carry out the transformations in the reverse order. Mark the image of A and label it A"

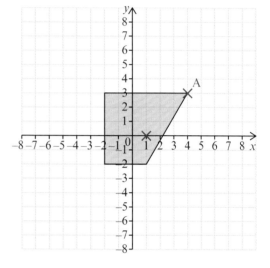

17 Find a combination of two transformations that will map these triangles onto each other.

a A onto C

b A onto D

c B onto C

d D onto A

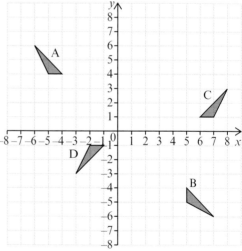

18 Write the single equivalent transformation for each of these repeated transformations. Give examples to show your answers are correct.

a Two rotations about the same centre

b Two translations

c Reflection in two parallel lines

d Reflection in two perpendicular lines

explanation 5a   explanation 5b

19 These shapes have
different symmetry
properties.

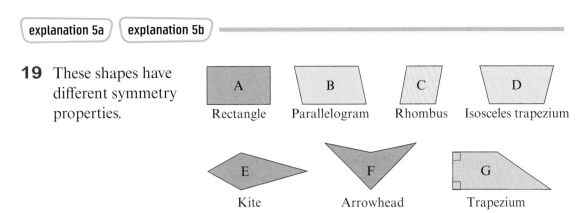

Copy and complete
this symmetry table
for the shapes.

		Number of lines of symmetry		
		0	1	2
Rotation	None		D	
symmetry	Order 2			

20 Copy these shapes.

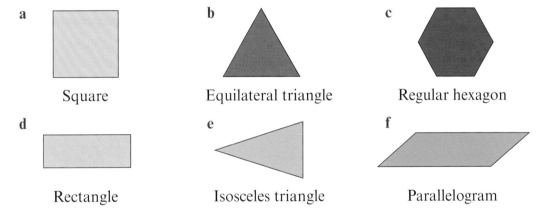

i Mark any lines of symmetry on each shape.

ii State the order of rotation symmetry of each shape.

21 State the order of rotation symmetry of these shapes.

a regular pentagon   **b** regular octagon   **c** circle

22 The diagrams show incomplete mosaic patterns.
Each pattern has 4 coloured tiles missing.
Copy and complete the patterns so that they have
the stated symmetry properties.

a Two lines of reflection symmetry, and rotation symmetry of order 2.

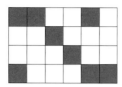

b One line of reflection symmetry, and rotation symmetry of order 1.

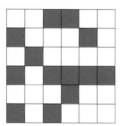

explanation 6

23 Sketch these shapes and draw the planes of symmetry on them.
You might want to draw them more than once.

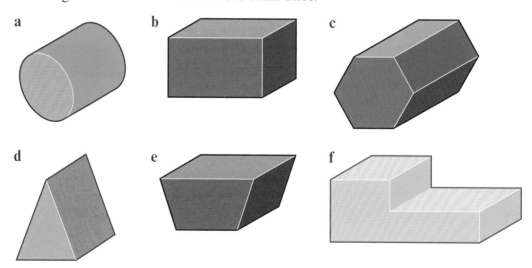

24 A cube has 9 planes of symmetry. Draw diagrams to show them.

Enlargement

- Enlarging an object with positive and negative scale factors
- Describing enlargements
- Determining scale factors

Keywords

You should know

explanation 1a   explanation 1b

1 Calculate each scale factor of enlargement.

a

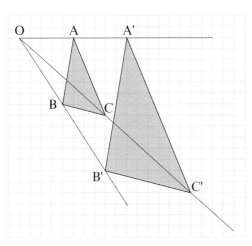

b

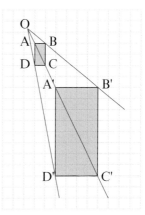

2 In each diagram, an object and a centre of enlargement, O, are shown.
Copy each diagram and enlarge the object by the given scale factor.

a Enlargement scale factor 3

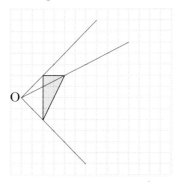

b Enlargement scale factor 5

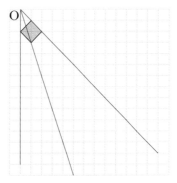

3 Copy these diagrams and enlarge each object by the scale factor shown. The centre of enlargement is marked O.

a Enlargement scale factor 2

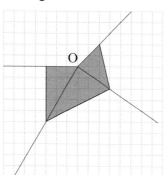

b Enlargement scale factor 2

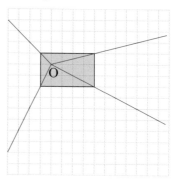

4 An object and its image are shown on each of the axes.

   i What are the coordinates of the centre of each enlargement?

   ii What is the scale factor of each enlargement?

a

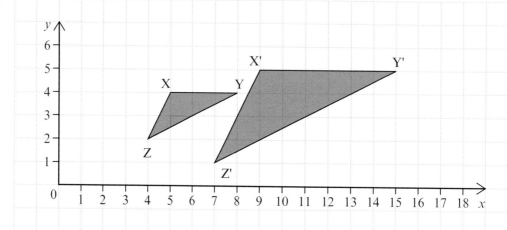

b

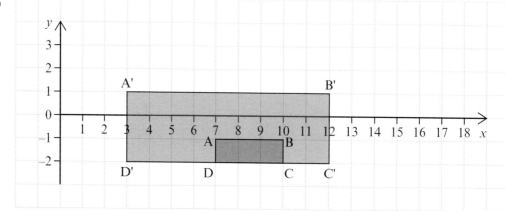

5 The diagram below shows object 1 and several enlargements.
Image 2 is an enlargement of object 1 by scale factor 2. Image 3 is an enlargement of object 1 by scale factor 3 etc. The centre of enlargement is at the origin.

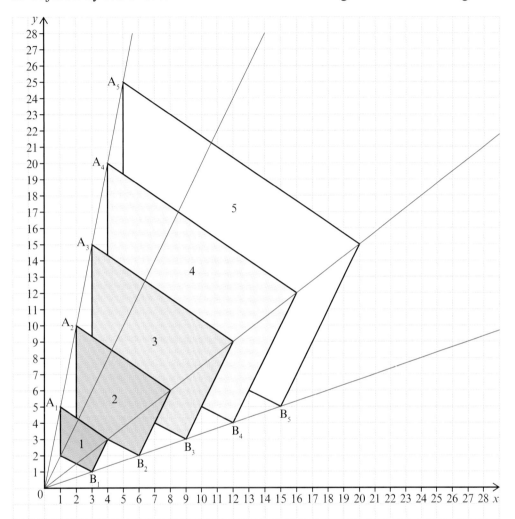

a What are the coordinates of A_1, A_2, A_3, A_4 and A_5?

b Predict the coordinates of A_6 and A_{10}. What are the coordinates of A_n?

c What are the coordinates of B_1, B_2, B_3, B_4 and B_5?

d Predict the coordinates of B_6 and B_{10}. What are the coordinates of B_n?

e An image of object 1 has coordinates (15, 75) for the A vertex.
What is the scale factor of the enlargement?

f What do you notice about the length of the sides of object 1 compared to the corresponding sides of the images?

g What do you notice about corresponding angles in object 1 and the images?

explanation 2

6 In each diagram, an object and a centre of enlargement, O, are shown.

Copy each diagram and enlarge it by the scale factor stated.

a

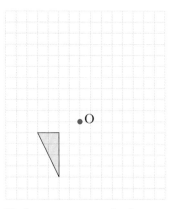

Enlargement scale factor −2

b

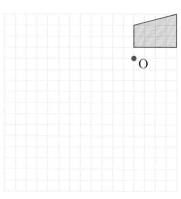

Enlargement scale factor −3

c

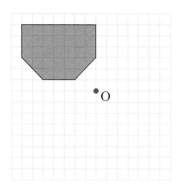

Enlargement scale factor −1

d

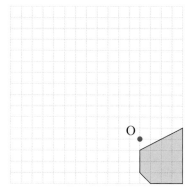

Enlargement scale factor −3

7 In these diagrams, shape A is mapped onto image A' by an enlargement.
Work out the scale factor of these enlargements.

a

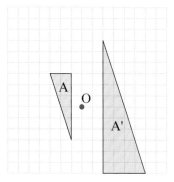

b

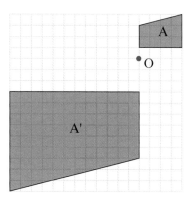

Surveys

- Knowing the different forms that data can take
- Testing a hypothesis
- Identifying inappropriate questions in a survey
- Sampling a population
- Using a two-way grouped frequency table to record data

Keywords

You should know

explanation 1

1 Decide which of the following types of data are qualitative and which are quantitative.

   a   The number of pupils in your class

   b   The hair colour of pupils in your class

   c   The amount of time spent doing homework

   d   The weight of pupils' school bags

   e   The temperature of your classroom

   f   Your friend's opinions on the TV they watched last night

   g   The taste of the food that you ate for dinner last night

   h   The price of a bus ticket

2 For each activity describe one variable that is

      i a quantitative measure   ii a qualitative measure

   a   Paul does a crossword each day.

   b   Maria chooses a pair of trainers.

   c   Ahmed plays a computer game.

   d   Zak cycles to school each day.

   e   Amy's dad went shopping on Saturday.

   f   Pedro's grandmother sent him a parcel for his birthday.

   g   Carla's class went on a school trip yesterday.

   h   Simon ate a cake for lunch.

3 Decide whether each variable is a discrete
or a continuous measure.

   a   The temperature of your classroom

   b   The shoe size of pupils in your class

   c   The amount of pocket money received by pupils each week

   d   The height of teachers in your school

   e   The weight of school bags carried by pupils in your class

   f   The number of pages in a maths textbook

   g   The time it takes pupils to get to school in the morning

   h   The speed of runners in a 100 m race

   i   The speed at which secretaries can type

   j   A person's age

(explanation 2a) (explanation 2b) (explanation 2c)

4 Data needs to be collected to test these theories.

Write the following for each hypothesis.

   i   A description of data that could be collected to test the hypothesis.

   ii   A source for the data and whether it is a primary or secondary source.

   a   Boys are taller than girls at secondary school.

   b   Most people in the UK have internet access at home.

   c   People recycle half of their household waste.

   d   Sporty pupils have faster reaction times than non-sporty pupils.

   e   Girls spend longer on homework than boys at secondary school.

   f   Parents of pupils in your school believe that more homework should be set.

   g   Children don't like to eat vegetables.

   h   People prefer to go abroad for their summer holidays.

   i   A cup of tea cools down more quickly if it is in a smaller cup.

5 Children's eating habits are being surveyed.

    i Identify what is wrong with each question.

    ii Suggest a better way to ask each question.

a Are you fat?   Yes ☐ No ☐ Not sure ☐

b What is your favourite food?   Pizza ☐ Burger ☐ Other ☐

c How old are you?   1−5 ☐ 5−10 ☐ 10−15 ☐ 15−20 ☐

d Do you like fruit and vegetables?   Yes ☐ No ☐

e What is your favourite TV programme?

f Fried food is bad for you. Do you like fried food?   Yes ☐ No ☐ Some ☐

g On average how many calories do you eat a day?

h How much do you weigh?   Less than 20 kg 20 kg−40 kg Over 8 stone

6 Sanjay and Katy want to know what music pupils in their school listen to. Sanjay decided to ask five of his friends and Katy decided to ask $\frac{3}{4}$ of the pupils in every class.

What is wrong with these samples and how could they be improved?

7 The school canteen wants to conduct a survey to decide what to sell at break and lunchtime. It is not possible to ask every pupil. Suggest a way pupils could be sampled.

> Remember to try to avoid bias in your sample.

8 A political party wants to know the voting intentions of adults in your area. Suggest a way in which the local population could be sampled.

9 For each of these surveys

    i identify the population

    ii suggest how you could select a sample

a Find out how pupils in your school travel to school.

b Find out how much people paid for their train tickets on a particular train.

c Find out how much people pay for their train tickets one day.

d Find out about local views on a housing development to be built in the area.

explanation 3a explanation 3b

10 Carry out an experiment to see if a drawing pin is more likely to land point up or point down when dropped.

a Draw a suitable table for recording the results.

b Carry out 50 trials and record the results in your table.

c Based on your results, explain whether you think a drawing pin is more likely to land point up or point down.

d Give two factors which you think may affect the outcome of the results.

11 A survey is to be carried out in order to compare the heights of boys and girls in your class. These are three possible tables in which to record the results.

Height (cm)	Number of girls	Number of boys
135		
136		
137		
138		
139		
140		
141		
142		
143		
144		
145		
146		
147		
etc		

Height (cm)	Number of girls	Number of boys
120−130		
130−140		
140−150		
150−160		
160−170		
170−180		

Height (cm)	Number of girls	Number of boys
$120 < h \leq 130$		
$130 < h \leq 140$		
$140 < h \leq 150$		
$150 < h \leq 160$		
$160 < h \leq 170$		
$170 < h \leq 180$		

a Which table is the most appropriate? Give reasons for your answer and explain why the other tables are not appropriate.

b Collect the heights of the pupils in your class and record them in the table.

c Comment on the results of your data collection.

12 A survey is to be carried out to find out approximately how long it takes pupils to travel to school and also how they travel to school each morning. Here are three possible tables in which to record the results.

Time (min)	Walk	Bus	Car	Taxi	Bicycle	Other
$0 < T \leq 5$						
$5 < T \leq 15$						
$15 < T \leq 17$						
$17 < T \leq 25$						
$25 < T \leq 50$						

Time (min)	Walk	Bus	Car	Taxi	Bicycle	Other
$0 < T \leq 10$						
$10 < T \leq 20$						
$20 < T \leq 30$						
$30 < T \leq 40$						
$40 < T \leq 50$						

Time (min)	Walk	Bus	Car	Taxi	Bicycle	Other
0−10						
10−20						
20−30						
30−40						
40−50						

a Which of the three tables is the most appropriate to use?
Give reasons for your answer.

b Carry out the survey with pupils in your class and record the results in the table.

c What conclusions can you draw from the data you have collected?

Analysing data (1)

- Understanding that statistics can be misleading
- Constructing a stem and leaf diagram
- Calculating the range, mean, median and mode from a stem and leaf diagram

Keywords

You should know

explanation 1a   explanation 1b

1   These are the masses in kilograms of 15 rugby players.

81, 110, 92, 95, 115, 118, 99, 95, 100, 102, 88, 89, 100, 111, 103

Work out these statistics for the data.

a   the range   b   the mode

c   the mean   d   the median

2   An Olympic 100 m sprinter ran these times, measured in seconds, in her last 8 competitive races.

12.82, 12.79, 12.02, 12.01, 12.88, 12.05, 12.52, 11.99

Work out these statistics for the data.

a   the range   b   the mode   c   the mean   d   the median

3   The mean of these numbers is 6. Calculate the value of x.

3, 8, 15, 7, x, 1

4   The median of these numbers is 8. Work out the value of m.

m, 20, 1, 3, 11, 6

5   These integers are written in ascending order.

6, 7, 7, 8, a, b, 19, 20

a   The mean of the eight numbers is 12. Calculate the possible values of a and b.

b   It is also known that the median of the eight numbers is 11.
    What are the only possible values for a and b?

6 The five players in a 5-a-side hockey team have these masses in kilograms.

60, 64, 58, 57, 61

a Calculate the total mass of the five players.

b Calculate the mean mass of the five players.

c The mean mass of the five players and the substitute is 61 kg.
  Calculate the mass of the substitute.

7 Peter and Amelia, play three games. Some of their scores are given in the table.
Their scores have the same mean. The range of Peter's scores is twice that of
Amelia's scores. Copy and complete the table.

Peter		44	
Amelia	38	45	49

explanation 2

8 Assad scored these marks out of 20 in his last eight maths tests.

4, 5, 20, 20, 3, 6, 2, 7

a Calculate these averages for the data.

  i the mean   ii the median   iii the mode

b Assad says that his average test score is 20. Is this true?

c In this case, which average is the best indicator of his results?
  Give reasons for your answer.

9 A manufacturer of batteries tests the life of the
batteries by testing ten of them.
Here are the number of hours each battery lasted.

14.5, 16.2, 17.1, 3.3, 16.0, 17.2, 17.8, 3.3, 18.1, 17.0

a Find these averages for the ten batteries tested.
  Give your answers in hours and minutes.

  i the mean   ii the median   iii the mode

b A rival battery manufacturer claims that these results
  show that on average the batteries only last 3.3 hours.
  Is this claim true? Give reasons for your answer.

c Explain, giving reasons, which is the most useful form of average for this data.

explanation 3

10 The shoe sizes of 30 pupils in a class are shown in the bar chart.

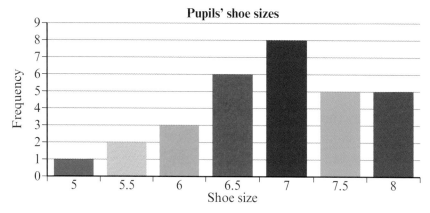

Pupils' shoe sizes

a How many pupils have a shoe size of 6?

b Calculate the mean shoe size of the 30 pupils.

c Calculate the median shoe size of the pupils.

d What is the modal shoe size of the pupils?

11 Reviewers were asked to preview a film and give it a rating from 1 to 5.
A score of 1 meant it was awful and 5 meant it was excellent. Their responses
are shown in the bar-line chart.

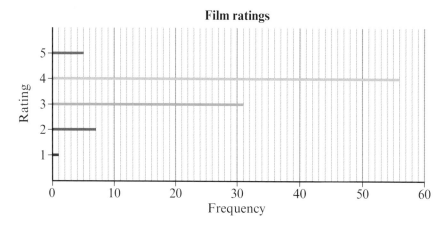

Film ratings

a How many people took part in the survey?

b How many people rated the film excellent?

c Calculate the mean rating for the film.

d Find the median rating for the film.

e What is the modal rating for the film?

explanation 4

12 25 caterpillars were measured.
Their lengths in millimetres are shown in this stem and leaf diagram.

```
0 | 9
1 | 2 2 4 7 9
2 | 1 1 3 4 5 5 7 8 8 9        Key: 2|1 represents a length of 21 mm
3 | 3 3 4 5 6 6 6
4 | 1 1
```

a Write the length of the shortest and the longest caterpillars measured.

b Find the modal caterpillar length.

c What is the median caterpillar length?

The caterpillars were fed for 2 weeks and their lengths recorded again.
It was found that all their lengths had increased by 5 mm.
How will this affect these statistics?

d the range of the lengths

e the modal length

f the mean and median length

13 20 girls and 20 boys sat the same maths test. These are their results out of 50.

Girls: 28, 32, 26, 21, 33, 33, 42, 7, 12, 14, 28, 50, 48, 14, 20, 38, 33, 32, 27, 22
Boys: 37, 26, 32, 32, 27, 2, 36, 7, 27, 33, 33, 36, 5, 7, 37, 36, 12, 31, 32, 12

a Draw a stem and leaf diagram for the girls' results and another for the boys' results.

b Write the modal results for the girls and for the boys.

c Calculate the median result for the girls and for the boys.

d Calculate the range of the girls' results and the range of the boys' results.

e Calculate the mean result for the girls and the mean result for the boys.

f Use your answers to write a short paragraph comparing the girls' and boys' results.

14 This back-to-back stem and leaf diagram shows the heights of two varieties of sunflower.

Calculate the mean and median heights of each variety of sunflower.

```
        Variety A              Variety B
        9 6 6 4 | 12 | 8
          8 5 0 | 13 | 1 6 9
  9 7 5 5 3 2 2 | 14 | 1 3 7 8
      8 7 3 1 0 | 15 | 2 6 6 8 9
              2 | 16 | 2 2 4 7 7
                | 17 | 3 5
```

Key   13|1 represents a height of 131 cm for variety B
       5|13 represents a height of 135 cm for variety A

15 The table shows times in seconds in the semi-finals and final for the men's 100 m at a major athletics tournament.

	Position							
	1	**2**	**3**	**4**	**5**	**6**	**7**	**8**
Semi-final 1 time (s)	9.95	9.97	9.97	10.02	10.12	10.22	10.28	10.28
Semi-final 2 time (s)	10.07	10.09	10.11	10.22	10.28	10.29	10.32	10.35
Final time (s)	9.85	9.86	9.87	9.89	9.94	10.00	10.10	10.11

a Copy and complete the back-to-back stem and leaf diagram below.

```
        Final                Semi-final
              | 10.3 |
              | 10.2 |
              | 10.1 |
              | 10.0 |
              |  9.9 | 5 7 7
         6 5  |  9.8 |
```

Key   9.9|5 represents 9.95 s in the semi-final
       5|9.8 represents 9.85 s in the final

b By carrying out appropriate calculations comment on any differences in the distributions of the results for the semi-finals and the final.

Representing data

- Drawing a pie chart by calculating the degrees for each sector
- Drawing bar charts or frequency diagrams as appropriate for discrete and continuous data
- Drawing and interpreting line graphs
- Drawing and interpreting scatter graphs

Keywords

You should know

explanation 1

1 The 20 pupils in a class were asked how many brothers or sisters they had. The results are shown in the table.

Number of brothers or sisters	0	1	2	3	4	5
Frequency	3	5	7	2	2	1

a How many degrees will represent each pupil in a pie chart?

b How many degrees will represent pupils who have 4 brothers or sisters?

c Copy and complete the table.

Number of brothers or sisters	0	1	2	3	4	5
Frequency	3	5	7	2	2	1
Angle						

d Draw a fully labelled pie chart to show the data clearly.

2 90 people were asked which television channel they watch the most. Their replies are shown in the table.

TV Channel	BBC1	BBC2	ITV1	Channel 4	Satellite	None	Unsure
Frequency	28	5	21	8	14	2	12
Angle							

a Copy and complete the table.

b Draw a pie chart to display the results of the survey.

3 A class of 30 pupils was asked which school lesson was their favourite.
The results are shown in the table.

Subject	English	Maths	Science	P.E.	Drama	Other
Frequency	2	10	6	7	3	2

a How many degrees in a pie chart will represent each pupil?

b How many degrees in a pie chart will represent the pupils who said maths
was their favourite subject?

c Draw and label a pie chart to display the results of the survey.

4 36 pupils in one year were asked what
animal was their favourite pet.
The pie chart shows the results from
the survey.

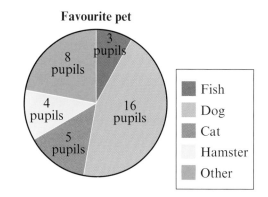

Favourite pet

a How many degrees represents
one pupil?

b How many degrees of the pie chart
represent pupils who said dogs were
their favourite pet?

c What fraction of pupils said hamsters were their favourite pet?
Give your answer in its simplest form.

5 The pie chart shows the results of a
survey to find out how people usually
travel to their local shopping centre.
180 people were questioned.

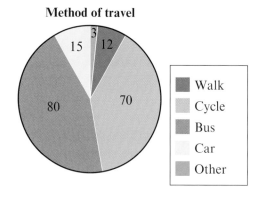

Method of travel

a How many degrees represent each
person in the survey?

b How many degrees of the pie chart
represent those who usually travel
by bus?

c What fraction of people surveyed said they usually cycle?
Give your answer in its simplest form.

explanation 2a   explanation 2b

6 A coffee shop carried out a survey to see what types of coffee their customers like drinking. The table shows the results.

Type of coffee	Cappuccino	Latte	Filter	Espresso	Other
Frequency	29	21	12	8	10

   a How many people were surveyed in total?

   b Construct a bar chart to show this data.

   c Draw a pie chart to show the data.

   d Which chart do you think shows the data more clearly?
Give a reason for your answer.

7 50 pupils are timed running 400 m. The results are grouped for display as a pie chart. The angle of each sector of the pie chart is shown in the table.

Time (s)	$60 \le T < 70$	$70 \le T < 80$	$80 \le T < 90$	$90 \le T < 100$	$100 \le T < 110$
Angle	14.4°	43.2°	201.6°	93.6°	7.2°

   a Explain what is meant by the time $90 \le T < 100$.

   b Calculate the frequency of each group.

   c Draw a frequency diagram for these results.

8 This frequency diagram shows the times that pupils in a class arrived at school one morning.

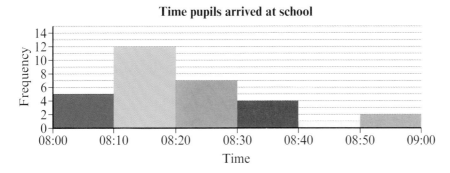

Time pupils arrived at school

   a How many pupils arrived before 08.20?

   b How many pupils arrived between 08.30 and 08.50?

   c How many pupils are there in the class?

9 Some of the world's mountains that are higher than 8000 m are listed in the table.

Mountain peak	Location	Height (m)
Everest	China/Nepal/Tibet	8850
K2	Pakistan/China	8611
Kanchenjunga	India/Nepal	8586
Lhotse I	China/Nepal/Tibet	8516
Makalu I	China/Nepal/Tibet	8463
Cho Oyu	China/Nepal/Tibet	8201
Dhaulagiri	Nepal	8167
Nanga Parbat	Pakistan	8163
Annapurna	Nepal	8091
Gasherbrum I	Pakistan/China	8068
Broad Peak	Pakistan/China	8047
Gasherbrum II	Pakistan/China	8035
Shisha Pangma	China	8013

a Copy and complete the grouped frequency table.

Height (m)	Frequency
$8000 \leq H < 8200$	
$8200 \leq H < 8400$	
$8400 \leq H < 8600$	
$8600 \leq H < 8800$	
$8800 \leq H < 9000$	

b Draw a frequency diagram showing the heights of the world's tallest mountains.

c Which is the modal height group?

explanation 3

10 The graph shows the temperature in degrees Celsius (°C) at a holiday resort over a 24-hour period.

Temperature readings were taken every 4 hours.

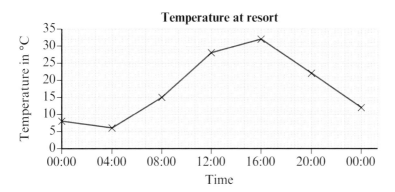

a   What was the temperature at noon?

b   What was the lowest temperature recorded over the 24-hour period?

c   A tourist at the resort claims that she recorded a temperature of 35°C at 14:00. Look at the graph and decide whether this is possible. Explain your answer.

11 A class at a primary school decide to see how many millimetres of rain fall over a ten-week period. A reading for the total rainfall is recorded every seven days. The results are shown in the table.

Days	7	14	21	28	35	42	49	56	63	70
Total rainfall (mm)	2	2	8	10	10	10	23	25	26	28

a   Draw a line graph to show the total amount of rainfall over the ten-week period.

b   In which weeks was there no rain?
Explain your answer.

c   In which week was there the most rain?
Explain your answer.

d   Calculate the average weekly rainfall during the ten-week period.

e   From your graph estimate the total amount of rain that had fallen by the 45th day.

explanation 4a | explanation 4b | explanation 4c | explanation 4d

12 The table shows the weights and ages of 10 infant girls.

Age (months)	22	15	7	11	20	18	14	12	6	10
Weight (kg)	11.0	9.4	7.9	9.6	10.2	10.3	8.9	8.9	7.5	8.5

a Plot the points on a scatter graph and draw a line of best fit.

b Is there a correlation between an infant girl's age and her weight?

c Use your graph to predict the weight of an 8-month-old infant girl.

d Should the line of best fit for this data be extended to predict the weight of a 25-year-old woman? Give reasons for your answer.

13 The engine size, in cubic centimetres, and average petrol consumption, in kilometres per litre, of 10 cars is given in the table.

Engine size (cc)	1000	900	1300	3000	2200	4500	800	1600	1100	1800
Average petrol consumption (kpl)	17	19	12.5	9	11.5	3.5	20	14	16.5	12

a Plot the points on a scatter graph and draw a line of best fit.

b Describe the type of correlation shown by the graph.

c Use your graph to predict the fuel consumption of a car with an engine size of 1500 cc.

14 15 pupils sat both a maths test and a science test.
Their percentage scores are shown in the table.

Maths %	98	55	27	38	82	77	64	12	62	68	84	55	36	90	60
Science %	88	60	34	38	75	81	70	20	65	55	92	60	30	100	72

a Draw a scatter graph of science results plotted against maths results.

b Does the graph show a correlation between the results?

c Draw a line of best fit for the results.

d A 16th pupil also sat both tests. If his score was 70% on the maths test estimate, using the line of best fit, his score for the science test.

e The teacher marks the science test and says that the pupil got 24%. Is this possible in light of the result you estimated for part **d**?

15 A motorist had 60 litres of petrol in her car when she set off on a journey. Every 100 km she recorded the number of litres of petrol still in her tank. The readings are given in the table.

Distance (km)	0	100	200	300	400	500	600	700	800
Petrol in tank (litres)	60	55	48	42	35	27	21	15	9

  a Draw a scatter graph of amount of petrol left against distance travelled.

  b Does the graph show a correlation between the results?

  c Draw a line of best fit for the results.

  d Use your line of best fit to estimate the amount of petrol in the tank when she had travelled 220 km.

16 Describe the type of correlation you would expect to see between each pair of variables. Give reasons for your answers.

  a The amount of pocket money a child receives and the amount they spend on sweets.

  b The age of children and their height.

  c The outside temperature and the amount of gas used for heating.

  d The price of a certain pair of trainers and the number of pairs of those trainers sold.

  e The weight of a pupil and their result in a maths test.

  f The number of cigarettes smoked and the risk of contracting lung cancer.

  g The number of years a person spends in full-time education and the starting salary of their first job.

  h The age of a second-hand car and its selling price.

Interpreting data

- Interpreting different types of graph
- Giving reasons to justify your answers
- Deciding whether a graph displays its data clearly

explanation 1

1 This graph shows crime statistics for vehicle theft since 1981.

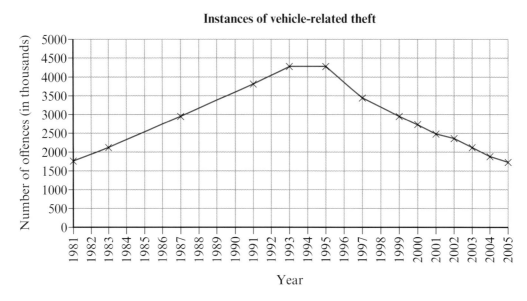

Instances of vehicle-related theft

a Approximately how many vehicle-related thefts were reported in 2005?

b Which years showed the highest theft figures?

c Write a short paragraph describing what the graph shows.

d Give a possible reason for the drop in vehicle-related thefts since 1995.

e This comment was made about the graph.

Although the number of car crimes was the same in 2005 as it was in 1981, in real terms, compared to the number of cars, this indicates a drop in car crime.'

Explain in your own words what you think this means.

2 The graphs show the overall crime figures between April 2005 and March 2006 for Region A and Region B compared to the national averages.

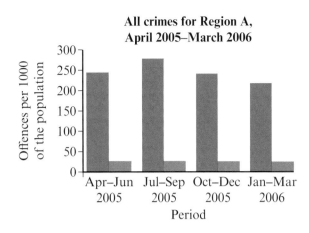

All crimes for Region A, April 2005–March 2006

Key — Chosen Region

— National average

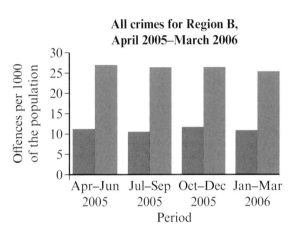

All crimes for Region B, April 2005–March 2006

a Approximately how many offences on average were committed per thousand of the population nationally between January and March 2006?

b Approximately how many offences were committed per thousand of the population in Region B between January and March 2006?

c Approximately how many offences were committed per thousand of the population in Region A between January and March 2006?

d Write a short paragraph describing any similarities and differences between the crime figures for the two regions.

e Explain whether you think the graphs are clear. Justify your answer.

f The y-axis on both graphs represents 'offences per 1000 of the population'. Explain in your own words what this means.

g In Region A between April and June 2005, the number of offences per 1000 of the population was approximately 250. Does this mean that nearly $\frac{1}{4}$ of the population of Region A committed an offence during that time?

3 These graphs show the 2007 population pyramids for two countries.
The numbers in the middle of the pyramid represent the ages of the population.

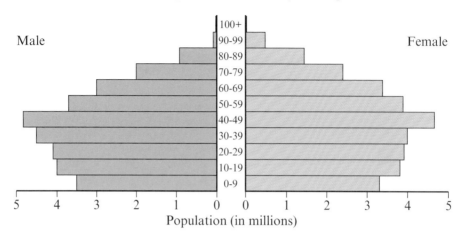

Population pyramid for a country in Europe

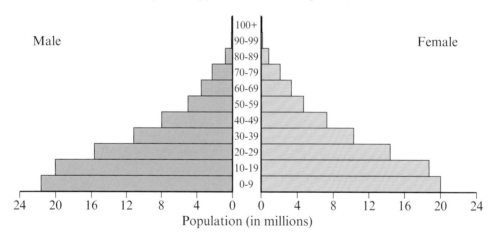

Population pyramid for a country in Asia

a When you look quickly at the graphs you might believe that there are more people in the European country than the Asian country.
Explain how you think this mistake could occur.

b Approximately how many 0–9 year old girls were there in the Asian country in 2007?

c Approximately how many 0–9 year old girls were there in the European country in 2007?

d In the Asian country which age group had the most people?

e In the European country which age group had the most people?

f Write a short paragraph describing some of the differences and similarities between the two graphs.

4 These graphs show the numbers of unemployed males and females taken from Census data for a city in 1931 and 2001.

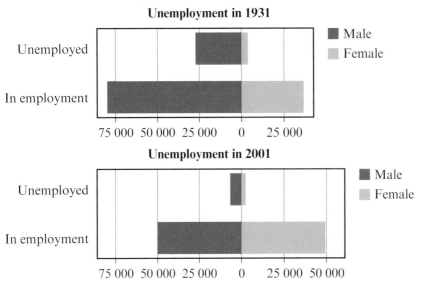

a Approximately how many women were in employment in 1931?

b Approximately how many men were in employment in 1931?

c Approximately what percentage of those employed in 1931 were women?

d Approximately what percentage of those employed in 2001 were women?

e Write a short paragraph commenting on the similarities and differences between the data for the two years shown.

5 This scatter graph compares the height and foot length of some pupils.

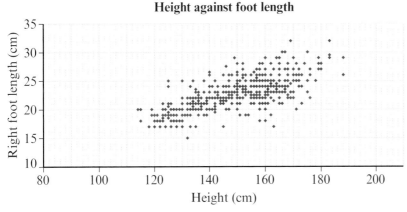

a What type of correlation, if any, does the scatter graph show between a pupil's height and foot length?

b Measure your own height and the length of your right foot. Does your data 'fit' with the data shown in the graph?

175

Order of operations

- Working out more complex calculations involving brackets and powers
- Understanding that multiplying by a number does not always produce a bigger answer
- Understanding that dividing by a number does not always produce a smaller answer

Keywords

You should know

explanation 1

1 Calculate these without using a calculator.

a $4 + 5^2$

b $(4 + 5)^2$

c $4^2 + 5^2$

d $\dfrac{13 - 3^2}{5}$

e $\dfrac{(13 - 3)^2}{5}$

f $\left(\dfrac{13 - 3}{5}\right)^2$

g $16 - 2 \times 4$

h $(16 - 2) \times 4$

i $24 \div 3 + 5$

j $24 \div (3 + 5)$

k $(36 \div 6 + 12) \div 4$

l $36 \div (6 + 12 \div 4)$

m $36 \div 6 + 12 \div 4$

n $36 \div (6 + 12) \div 4$

o $(36 \div 6) + (12 \div 4)$

2 Calculate these without using a calculator.

a $12 - 3 \times 2$

b $(12 - 3) \times 2$

c $8^2 - 14 \div 2$

d $(8^2 - 14) \div 2$

e $(15 - 5)^2 \times 2 + 8$

f $15 - 5^2 \times (2 + 8)$

g $15 - 5^2 \times 2 + 8$

h $15 - (5^2 \times 2 + 8)$

i $(15 - 5^2) \times 2 + 8$

3 Insert brackets in these calculations, if necessary, to make them correct.

a $6 + 24 \div 6 + 4 = 14$

b $6 + 24 \div 6 + 4 = 9$

c $6 + 24 \div 6 + 4 = 3$

d $6 + 24 \div 6 + 4 = 8.4$

e $16 + 4^2 \times 8 - 3 = 3197$

f $16 + 4^2 \times 8 - 3 = 141$

g $16 + 4^2 \times 8 - 3 = 96$

h $16 + 4^2 \times 8 - 3 = 160$

4 The perimeter, P, of the rectangle below is given by this formula.
$P = 2x + 2y$.

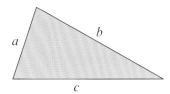

   a Write the formula for the perimeter of the rectangle using brackets.

   b Calculate the perimeter when $x = 6\,$cm and $y = 3.5\,$cm.

5 The perimeter, P, of this triangle is given by the formula $P = a + b + c$.

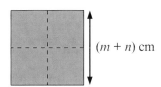

Write, using brackets, the formula for the perimeter of a triangle whose edges are double the length of these.

6 This square has sides of length $(m + n)$ cm.

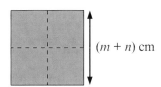

$(m + n)$ cm

   a Using brackets, write a formula for the perimeter, P, of the square.

   b Using brackets, write a formula for the area, A, of the square.

   c The square is divided into four equal parts as shown. Write an expression, using brackets, for the perimeter of each of the smaller squares.

   d Write an expression for the area of each of the smaller squares.

> explanation 2a   explanation 2b

7 Copy and complete these statements by inserting >, < or = in the spaces.

   a $7 \times 0.1 \,\square\, 7$
      b $6 \times 0.4 \,\square\, 6$
      c $8 \times 0.2 \,\square\, 0.2$

   d $15 \times 0.3 \,\square\, 15$
      e $12 \times 0.1 \,\square\, 1.2$
      f $0.3 \times 0.5 \,\square\, 0.3$

   g $25 \times 0.2 \,\square\, 5$
      h $0.2 \times 30 \,\square\, 30$
      i $0.4 \times 0.6 \,\square\, 0.6$

8 Work these out without using a calculator.

a 5×0.1 b 5×0.3 c 5×0.8

d 8×0.1 e 8×0.3 f 8×0.9

g 20×0.01 h 20×0.02 i 20×0.05

j 55×0.01 k 55×0.02 l 55×0.06

9 Copy and complete these statements by inserting $>$, $<$ or $=$ in the spaces.

a $8 \div 0.2 \,\square\, 8$ b $12 \div 0.5 \,\square\, 12$ c $20 \div 0.8 \,\square\, 20$

d $0.5 \div 0.1 \,\square\, 0.5$ e $5 \div 0.2 \,\square\, 25$ f $0.5 \div 5 \,\square\, 0.5$

10 Work these out without using a calculator.

a $5 \div 0.1$ b $5 \div 0.2$ c $5 \div 0.5$

d $2 \div 0.1$ e $20 \div 0.1$ f $200 \div 0.1$

g $100 \div 0.1$ h $10 \div 0.01$ i $1 \div 0.001$

11 a In your own words describe the effect of multiplying a positive number by a number that is between 0 and 1.

b What happens if you multiply a negative number by a number that is between 0 and 1?

12 a In your own words describe the effect of dividing a positive number by a number that is between 0 and 1.

b What happens if you divide a negative number by a number that is between 0 and 1?

13 For each statement below

   i decide whether it is true or false

   ii give an example to demonstrate your answer to part **i**

a Multiplying any number by a number greater than 1 gives a bigger answer.

b Multiplying a negative number by a number between 0 and 1 gives a bigger answer.

c Dividing a negative number by a number greater than 1 gives a smaller answer.

Checking

- Spotting incorrect answers in a number of different situations

Keywords

You should know

explanation 1

1 In each pair of calculations one is incorrect.
Without using a calculator, identify the incorrect calculation.
Give a reason for your choice.

a i $56 + 8 \div 8 = 8$ ii $56 + 8 \div 8 = 57$

b i $25 - 10 \times 2 = 30$ ii $25 - 10 \times 2 = 5$

c i $(14.1 - 3.8)^2 = 106.09$ ii $(14.1 - 3.8)^2 = 20.09$

d i $\dfrac{27.3 \times 2.9}{9.1} = 8.7$ ii $\dfrac{27.3 \times 2.9}{9.1} = 0.87$

e i $\dfrac{\sqrt{100 - 36}}{4} = 2$ ii $\dfrac{\sqrt{100 - 36}}{4} = 20$

f i $(20 - 15)^2 - 10 \div 5 = 3$ ii $(20 - 15)^2 - 10 \div 5 = 23$

g i $5 \times 4.9^2 = 600.25$ ii $5 \times 4.9^2 = 120.05$

h i $\dfrac{52 \div 5^2}{3.8} = 28.46$ ii $\dfrac{52 \div 5^2}{3.8} = 0.547$

2 Without using a calculator, pick out a possible answer to the calculation from
the numbers given. Give a reason for your choice.

a 58×60 i 3480   ii 348   iii 4080

b $4.98 \div 0.33$ i 1.66   ii 15.09   iii 0.92

c $327 \div 1.1$ i 297.27   ii 29.73   iii 327.11

d 1001×2.1 i 2001.1   ii 2102.1   iii 1999.1

3 a $\sqrt{x} = 22.5$.

  Which of these methods is correct for finding x?

  i $x = 2 \times 22.5$ **ii** $x = 22.5^2$ **iii** $x = \sqrt{22.5}$

b $p^2 = 2116$ and p is a positive number.

  Which of these methods is correct for finding p?

  i $p = 2116 \div 2$ **ii** $p = 2116^2$ **iii** $p = \sqrt{2116}$

c $(m - 25) \div 5 = 15$.

  Which of these methods is correct for finding m?

  i $m = 15 \times 5 + 25$ **ii** $m = (15 + 25) \times 5$ **iii** $m = 15 + 5$

4 a Ali did a survey of eye colours with the 25 pupils in his class.
  He produced this table of results showing the percentage in each category.

Eye Colour	Blue	Brown	Hazel	Green
Percentage	40%	30%	25%	15%

  Explain why these results must be incorrect.

b Sarah repeated the survey with the same 25 pupils.
  These are her results.

Eye Colour	Blue	Brown	Hazel	Green
Percentage	40%	30%	14%	16%

  Explain why her results must be incorrect as well.

c The survey was repeated in another class with 30 pupils.
  The results are shown below.

Eye Colour	Blue	Brown	Hazel	Green
Percentage	$43\frac{1}{3}\%$	$33\frac{1}{3}\%$	$13\frac{1}{3}\%$	10%

  Explain why these results could be correct.

5 These are the masses in kilograms of 10 pupils.

  45   38   52   55   51   48   50   49   41   53

  The mean mass was calculated as 56 kg.
  Without calculating the mean, explain why this value cannot possibly be correct.

Ratios

- Understanding the relationship between fractions and ratios
- Simplifying ratios
- Dividing a quantity in a given ratio
- Using the unitary method to solve problems involving ratio

Keywords

You should know

explanation 1

1 Write the proportion of each shape that is coloured, as a fraction in its simplest form.

a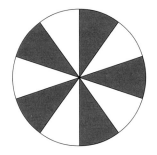

b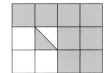

c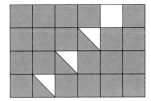

d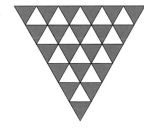

e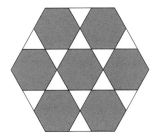

f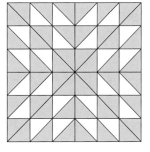

2 For each shape in question **1**, write the proportion that is coloured as a ratio, coloured : all tiles

3 The bar chart shows the number of hours spent on homework by a group of 24 pupils in one week.

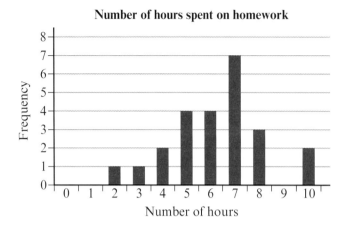

Number of hours spent on homework

a   What proportion of the pupils did exactly 5 hours?

Give your answer as a fraction in its simplest form.

b   What proportion of the pupils did 5 or more hours?

Give your answer as a fraction in its simplest form.

c   What is the ratio of pupils who did exactly 5 hours homework to pupils who spent other lengths of time doing homework?

d   What is the ratio of pupils who spent 5 or more hours on homework to pupils who spent fewer than 5 hours doing homework?

4 The pie chart shows the eye colour of a group of 36 people.

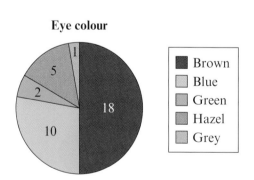

Eye colour

a   What proportion of the people have brown eyes?

b   What is the ratio of people with brown eyes to people with other coloured eyes?

c   What proportion of the people have either green or grey eyes?

d   What is the ratio of people with green or grey eyes to people with other coloured eyes?

explanation 2

5 Use the data on eye colour from question **4**.

   a What is the ratio of grey to hazel eyes in this group?
Express your ratio in its simplest form.

   b What is the ratio of green to brown eyes in this group?
Express your ratio in its simplest form.

   c Two of the eye colours in this group are in the ratio $9:5$.
Which two eye colours are these?

6 Simplify these ratios.

   a $4:2$ **b** $8:6$ **c** $8:12$ **d** $5:15$

   e $16:24$ **f** $18:27$ **g** $30:72$ **h** $33:6$

   i $21:56$ **j** $35:21$ **k** $21:28:35$ **l** $49:63:14$

7 Each pair of ratios is equivalent. Work out the values of the letters.

   a $1:2 = 3:x$ **b** $7:21 = p:42$ **c** $2:5 = n:25$

   d $15:y = 45:18$ **e** $a:9 = 40:72$ **f** $6:18 = 5:b$

   g $1:2:3 = 5:m:n$ **h** $3:5:6 = p:30:q$ **i** $d:3:7 = 16:12:e$

explanation 3

8 A model car is made to a scale of $1:50$.

   a The model has a length of $10\,\text{cm}$.
Calculate the length of the real car.
Give your answer in metres.

   b The real car has a height of $1.75\,\text{m}$.
Calculate the height of the model car.

9 In 2007, the Taipei Tower in Taiwan, was the world's tallest building, standing at a height of approximately 510 m.

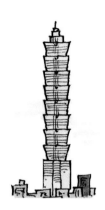

  a On a photograph the tower is 15 cm tall.

   What is the scale of the photo to the real tower?

   Write the ratio in its simplest form.

  b A poster is produced to a scale of 1 : 200.

   Calculate the height of the tower on the poster.

10 A map is drawn to a scale of 1 : 50 000.

  a Calculate the real distance when the distance on the map is 3 cm.

   Give your answer in metres.

  b Calculate the distance on the map, if a distance on the ground is 8 km.

   Give your answer in centimetres.

11 An architect produces a plan of a building to a scale of 1 : 25.

  a The height of the real building will be 8 m. Calculate the height of the building on the plan, giving your answer in centimetres.

  b The length of the building on the plan is 45 cm. Calculate the length of the actual building. Give your answer in metres.

12 Write each ratio in its simplest form.

  a 2 cm : 5 m   **b** 8 mm : 12 cm

  c 25 g : 3 kg   **d** 6 mm : 5 m

  e 4 mm : 1 km   **f** 15 kg : 2 tonnes

  g 125 g : 1 tonne   **h** 20 s : 5 min   **i** 5 s : 2 hours

  j 150 mm : 15 km   **k** 10 min : 3 days   **l** 40 ml : 10 litres

> Remember to change the quantities into the same units first.

explanation 4

13 A piece of string 24 cm long is divided into smaller pieces in these ratios.
Calculate the length of each of the smaller pieces.

    a 1:7   **b** 1:5   **c** 1:3   **d** 7:5   **e** 5:19

    f 41:7   **g** 1:2:3   **h** 3:5:4   **i** 38:7:3   **j** 35:35:2

14 A piece of wood 48 cm long is cut into smaller pieces in these ratios.
Calculate the length of each of the smaller pieces of wood.

    a 1:15   **b** 5:1   **c** 1:95   **d** 1:1:14

    e 1:2:3:6   **f** 2:10:25:59   **g** 6:8:5:3:2   **h** 10:12:16:34

15 Blue, white and yellow paint is mixed in the ratio 3:20:2.
The paint is sold in 5 litre containers.

Calculate the volume of each colour paint in the container.

    a White paint   **b** Blue paint   **c** Yellow paint

16 Fruit juice is made from mango, orange, apple and grape juice in the ratio
4:8:3:1. The juice is sold in 1 litre cartons.

    a Calculate the amount of mango juice in a carton.

    b Calculate the amount of apple juice in a carton.

    c A promotional carton is produced with 25% extra free.
       Calculate the amount of grape juice in a promotional carton.

17 P and Q are two chain wheels.
For every 2 complete rotations that
wheel P makes, wheel Q makes 7.

   a Calculate the number of rotations made
by wheel Q when wheel P makes
250 rotations.

   b Calculate the number of rotations made by wheel P when wheel Q makes
497 rotations.

   c If the combined number of rotations is 1620, calculate the number of
rotations made by each wheel.

18 A square has the same area as a rectangle.

The sides of the rectangle are in the ratio 9:4.
The perimeter of the rectangle is 130 cm.

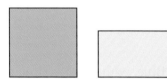

   a Calculate the lengths of the sides of
the rectangle.

   b Calculate the area of the rectangle.

   c Calculate the side length of the square.

   d Write down the ratio of the perimeters of the two shapes in the form
perimeter of square : perimeter of rectangle.
Give your answer in its simplest form.

*19 Two jars contain sweets. Jar X has red and white sweets in the ratio 1:5,
and jar Y has red and white sweets in the ratio 1:12.

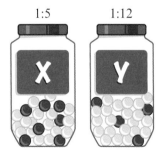

The two jars are then mixed together. Find the smallest number of sweets that
could have been in each jar if the red and white sweets are now in these ratios.
  a 1:6   **b** 1:7   **c** 1:8   **d** 1:9   **e** 1:10   **f** 1:4

Graphs of real-life situations

- Knowing the properties of direct proportionality
- Using graphs to find the relationship between two variables
- Writing a ratio in the form 1:n
- Converting a ratio to an equation linking two variables

Keywords

You should know

explanation 1a ⟋ explanation 1b

1 In February 2008, the exchange rate between pounds (£) and Japanese yen (¥) was approximately 1:210. Therefore £1 could be exchanged for ¥210.

 a Copy and complete the exchange rate table.

Pounds (£)	0	5	10	15	20
Japanese yen (¥)					

 b Plot a graph showing the relationship between pounds and yen.

2 In August 2007, the exchange rate between pounds (£) and euros (€) was approximately 2:3. Therefore £2 could be exchanged for 3€.

 a Copy and complete the following exchange rate table.

Pounds (£)	0	10	20	50	100
Euros (€)		15			

 b Plot a graph to show the relationship between pounds and euros.

 By February 2008, the exchange rate had changed and pounds to euros was approximately 1 : 1.35.

 c On the same axes plot the new graph showing the relationship between pounds and euros.

 d How many less euros would a person get for exchanging £300 in August 2007 compared with February 2008?

3 A car is driving at a constant speed. The table shows the total number of kilometres the car has travelled at different points in time.

Time (h)	0	1.5	3	4.5	6
Distance (km)		135		405	

a Calculate the speed, in km/h of the car.

b Copy and complete the table.

c Plot a graph showing the relationship between time and distance travelled.

d Use your graph to estimate the distance travelled after 3 hours 45 minutes.

explanation 2a   explanation 2b   explanation 2c

4 This graph can be used to convert between miles and kilometres.

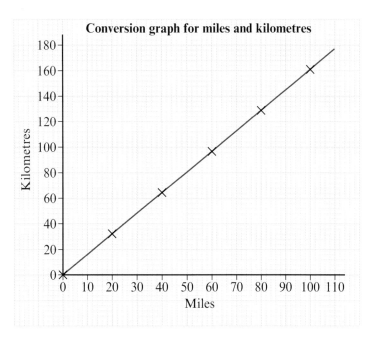

a From the graph find the number of kilometres equivalent to 100 miles.

b Find the number of kilometres in 1 mile.

c Calculate the number of kilometres equivalent to 70 miles.
Show your working clearly.

d Use the graph to help you find the number of miles equivalent to 250 km.
Show your working clearly.

5 Write each of the following ratios in the form $1:n$

a $2:5$ b $3:10$ c $4:5$ d $9:15$

e $15:6$ f $25:6$ g $1.5:1$ h $9:5$

6 The graph below shows the conversion between inches and centimetres.

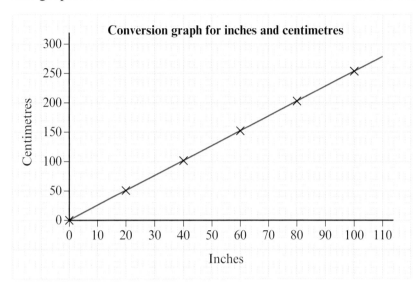

a   Use the graph to find the number of centimetres equivalent to 50 inches.

b   Calculate the number of centimetres equivalent to 1 inch.

c   Write the ratio number of inches : number of centimetres in the form $1:n$.

d   Calculate the number of centimetres equivalent to 85 inches.

e   Use the graph to find the number of inches equivalent to 100 cm.

f   Calculate the number of inches equivalent to 1 cm.

g   Write the ratio number of centimetres : number of inches in the form $1:n$.

h   Calculate the number of inches equivalent to 1.75 m.

7 The graph below shows the conversion between litres and pints.

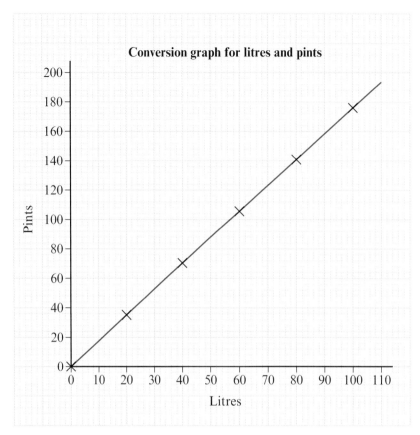

Conversion graph for litres and pints

a Use the graph to find the number of pints equivalent to 50 litres.

b Calculate the number of pints equivalent to 1 litre.

c Write the ratio number of litres : number of pints in the form 1 : n.

d Calculate the number of pints equivalent to 72 litres.

e Use the graph to help you find the number of litres equivalent to 1 pint.

f Write the ratio number of pints : number of litres in the form 1 : n.

g Write the relationship betwen a capacity in litres, L, and the equivalent capacity in pints, P, as a equation.

h In 1995, the average yearly milk yield for a dairy cow in the UK was 11 000 pints.
Convert the average yearly milk yield to litres.

8 An experiment is conducted to find the relationship between the mass, in grams, attached to a spring and its extension, measured in centimetres.
The apparatus is set up as shown.

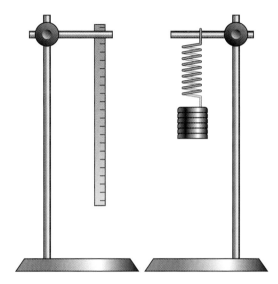

The results from the experiment are shown in the table below.

Mass (g)	Extension (cm)
0	0
10	2.1
20	3.9
30	6.2
50	10.3
100	18.8

a Plot a graph showing the results and draw a line of best fit.

b What is the approximate relationship between mass and extension?

c Write the relationship between the mass (M) and the extension (E) as an equation.

Formulae and expressions

- Simplifying more complex algebraic expressions involving brackets
- Forming algebraic expressions
- Multiplying a single term over a bracket
- Taking out a single term common factor

Keywords

You should know

explanation 1

1 In each algebra caterpillar, the expression in each section is the sum of the expressions in the previous two sections.

What are the missing expressions? Give each answer in its simplest form.

a
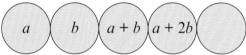

b
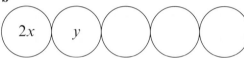

c
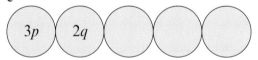

d
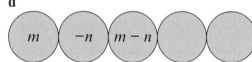

e
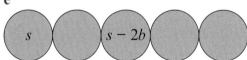

f
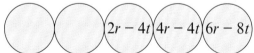

explanation 2a   explanation 2b

2 In an addition pyramid, the expression in each brick is the sum of the expressions in the two bricks beneath it.

Copy and complete each pyramid. Give each expression in its simplest form.

a
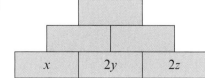

b
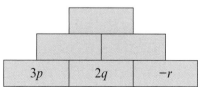

3 Copy and complete these addition pyramids. Simplify each expression.

a

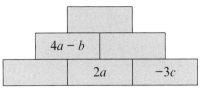

b

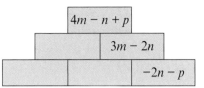

c

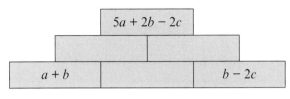

d

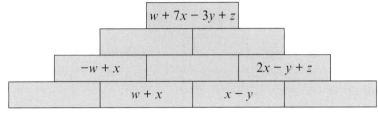

explanation 3

4 For each function machine, what is the output for each input?
Copy and complete each table. Write each answer in its simplest form.

a Input → × 2 → Output

	Input	Output
i	$3x + 2$	
ii	$\dfrac{x}{3}$	
iii	$a - 6$	
iv	$\dfrac{p - 4}{5}$	

b Input → + 1 → × 3 → Output

	Input	Output
i	$k - 1$	
ii	$\dfrac{m}{3}$	
iii	$-\dfrac{1}{3}(y + 3)$	
iv	$\dfrac{1 - u}{6}$	

5 Copy and complete each table. Give each answer in its simplest form.

a Input → $\div 2$ → $+ a$ → Output

Input	Output
$4a + 2b$	
$6 - a$	
$4(x - a)$	
$\dfrac{-4a + 8}{2}$	

(i, ii, iii, iv)

b Input → $\times 3$ → $- b$ → Output

Input	Output
$a + b$	
$\dfrac{b}{3}$	
$-b + 2$	
$\dfrac{b}{6}$	

(i, ii, iii, iv)

c Input → $+ 6$ → $\times q$ → Output

Input	Output
$2(q - 3)$	
$\dfrac{1}{q}$	
$\dfrac{p - 5q}{q}$	
$c - 3(b + 2)$	

(i, ii, iii, iv)

d Input → $- 2$ → $\div z$ → Output

Input	Output
$\dfrac{z + 4}{2}$	
$\dfrac{z}{2} + 4$	
$1 + \dfrac{az^3 + z}{z}$	
$\dfrac{x^2 - x(x - a)}{0.5ax}$	

(i, ii, iii, iv)

explanation 4a   explanation 4b

6 Multiply out these brackets.

a $4(x + 3)$ b $5(a - 1)$ c $3(2b - d)$

d $x(x + 2)$ e $2p(p - q)$ f $3r(2 + 4r)$

g $5x(x - y + 2z)$ h $m(m^2 - 2n)$ i $x^2(3 - x)$

7 Write an algebraic expression for the shaded area of each diagram.
Give your answers in simplified form.

a
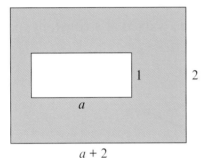

b
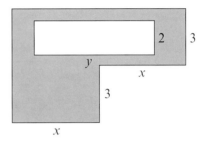

c
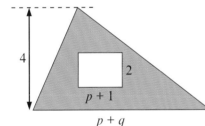

d
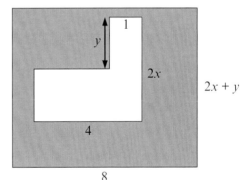

> **Remember**
> Area of a rectangle = length × width
> Area of a triangle = $\frac{1}{2}$ × base × height

8 Factorise these expressions as far as you can.

a $3x + 6$ b $12x - 6$ c $15p + 10q$

d $m^2 - 2m$ e $4x - x^2$ f $2p^2 - 4p$

g $x^2 - ax^2$ h $2m^3 + 3m^2$ i $2a^3 + a^2b^2 - 3a^2$

9 Factorise $3xy^2 + 4x^3y^2 - x^2y^3$ as far as possible.

Use your answer to simplify $\dfrac{3xy^2 + 4x^3y^2 - x^2y^3}{3 + 4x^2 - xy}$.

Using graphs

- Interpreting distance–time graphs
- Drawing graphs based on real situations
- Recognising that some graphs can be misleading
- Giving possible explanations for the shape of graphs

Keywords

You should know

explanation 1a   explanation 1b

1 The distance–time graph shows the distance Ben walked at a constant speed.

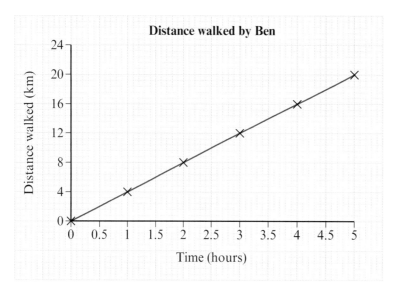

Distance walked by Ben

a How far did Ben walk in 5 hours?

b What was Ben's speed in kilometres per hour?

c Write an equation that links the distance Ben walked (d km) and the time he took (t hours).

d Ben continued to walk at this speed. Use your equation from part **c** to calculate how far Ben walked in 8 hours.

e Ben is going to do a walk for charity. The distance he has to walk is 34 km.

Estimate how long he will take to walk the 34 km.

2 Rebecca was at school and Arjun was at his house 8 km away.
Rebecca started cycling towards Arjun at a steady speed.
At the same time, Arjun started walking in the same direction at a steady speed.
This distance–time graph shows their distances from school.

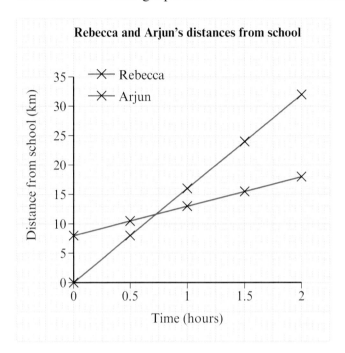

a Approximately how long did Rebecca take to overtake Arjun?

b Explain how you arrived at your answer to part **a**.

c How far did Rebecca cycle in 2 hours?

d What was Rebecca's speed in kilometres per hour?

e How far did Arjun walk in 2 hours?

f What was Arjun's speed?

g Write an equation that links Rebecca's distance from school (r km) with time (t hours).

h Write an equation that links Arjun's distance from school (a km) with time (t hours).

i When Rebecca overtakes Arjun, they are the same distance from school, so $r = a$. By solving an equation, calculate the time that Rebecca took to overtake Arjun. Give your answer to the nearest minute.

3 Gethin and Abbie were 12 km apart. They started walking at the same time and walked towards each other. Gethin set off from point O. The distance–time graph shows their distances from O.

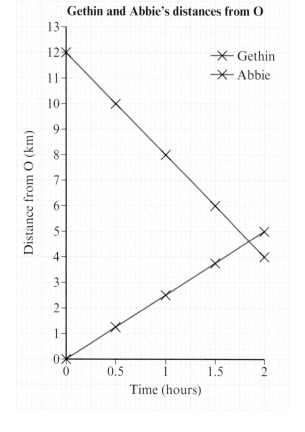

Gethin and Abbie's distances from O

a What do straight lines mean on a distance–time graph?

b How far had Gethin travelled after 2 hours?

c What was Gethin's speed?

d Write an equation that links Gethin's distance from O (g km) with time (t hours).

e What was Abbie's speed?

f Write an equation that links Abbie's distance from O (a km) with time (t hours).

g How far apart were Gethin and Abbie after 1 hour?

h By solving an equation, calculate how long it took Gethin and Abbie to pass each other.

4 A plumber charges a £50 call out fee and then £25 for each hour worked. The table shows the cost of hiring the plumber for different lengths of time.

Number of Hours	0	1	2	3	4
Cost (£)	50	75	100	125	150

a Plot a graph showing the cost (£C) of hiring the plumber against time (t hours).

b Write an equation that links the cost (£C) and the time (t hours).

c Use your equation to work out how much the plumber would charge for a job lasting 1 hour 45 minutes.

d How long would the plumber have worked if he charged £280 for a job?

5 Two removal companies give a family a quote for helping them move house.

Company A charges a fee of £100 and then £1.50 for each kilometre travelled.

Company B charges a fee of £150 and then £1.30 for each kilometre travelled.

a Copy and complete this table of removal costs.

Distance (km)	0	25	50	100	200	500
Charge Company A (£)	100.00					
Charge Company B (£)	150.00					

b On the same axes, plot a line graph showing the charges for each company.

c Estimate the distance for which both companies charge the same amount.

d Write an equation that links the charge (£A) and the distance (d km) for Company A.

e Write an equation that links the charge (£B) and the distance (d km) for Company B.

f Calculate the actual distance for which both companies charge the same amount. Use your equations from parts **d** and **e**.

6 These graphs show the profits (in millions of pounds) of two companies.

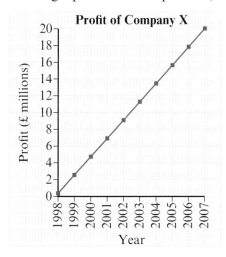

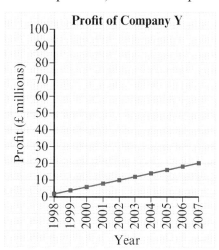

a Which company has had the steepest rise in profits over the 10 years?

b What was the profit of Company X in 2007?

c What was the profit of Company Y in 2007?

d Check your answer to part **a** by looking at your answers to parts **b** and **c**.

e Are the graphs misleading? Justify your answer.

explanation 2

7 Water is poured at the same constant rate into each of these five containers.

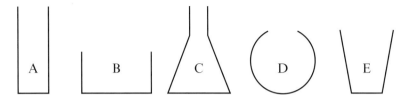

Here are three graphs that show how the depth of water changes with time.

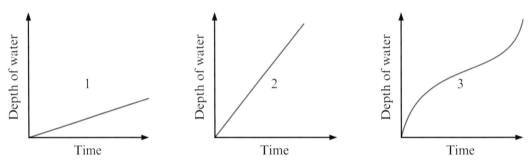

a Match three of the containers with their corresponding depth–time graphs.

b Sketch the graphs for the two remaining containers.

8 This graph shows the temperature of a pan of water used for cooking frozen peas.

Give a possible explanation for the shape of the graph.

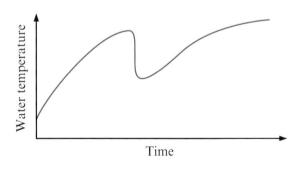

9 This graph shows the depth of water in a water barrel over a period of time.

Give a possible explanation for the shape of the graph.

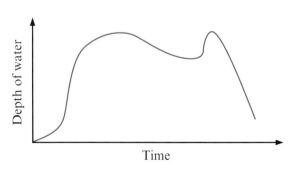

Scale drawing

- Converting lengths from scale drawings to real life, and vice versa
- Drawing diagrams to scale
- Interpreting diagrams drawn to scale
- Interpreting scaled areas

Keywords

You should know

explanation 1a explanation 1b

1 Boris draws a plan of his flat to a scale of 1:40.
He measures these lengths from the plan. Calculate the actual lengths in metres.

a Length of lounge: 12 cm

b Length of bathroom: 5.25 cm

2 In these questions, the plan lengths and the scales are given.
Calculate the actual lengths. Give your answers in metres.

a 5 cm, 1:50

b 11 mm, 1:25 000

c 7.5 cm, 3:1000

3 In these questions, the actual lengths and the scales are given.
Calculate the scaled lengths. Give your answers in centimetres.

a 120 m, 1:500

b 6.5 km, 1:50 000

c 120 mm, 3:5

4 On a map, the distance from Exeter to Cambridge is 16 cm and the distance
from Aberdeen to Cambridge is 34 cm.
Aidan knows that the real distance from Exeter to Cambridge is 400 km.

What is the scale of the map?
Find the real distance from Aberdeen to Cambridge.

5 A swimming pool is rectangular and has a length of 50 m and a width of 25 m.

a Draw a scale diagram of the pool. Use a scale of 1:1000.

b What is the area of the pool on the diagram?

c What is the actual area of the pool? Give your answer in

   i square metres

   ii square centimetres

6 The diagram shows a football pitch.

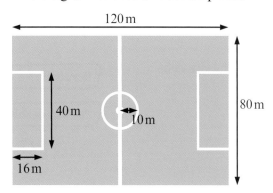

Draw a scale diagram of the football pitch, using a scale of 3:4000.

7 The diagram below shows a rectangular pool
20 m long by 10 m wide.
Rachel stands at R and Steve stands at S.

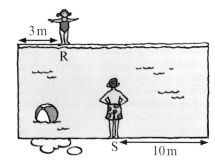

a Draw a scale diagram of the pool, using
1 cm for 2 m.

b Tom swims across the pool. He is always
the same distance from Rachel as from Steve.
Construct Tom's path across the pool.

> Draw the line segment RS. Every point
> on the perpendicular bisector of RS is
> equidistant from R and S.

8 A small rectangular swimming pool WXYZ is
7.5 m long and 5 m wide.

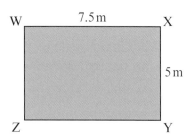

A girl sets off from corner Z and swims
towards the edge WX in such a way that she
bisects the angle WZY.

On arrival at the edge WX she turns and
heads directly towards the corner Y.

a Using a scale of 1:125, draw a scale diagram of the pool.

b Using a pair of compasses and a ruler, construct the path taken by the girl.

c By measuring the path taken, calculate the actual distance swum by the girl.

explanation 2

9 A plan of a classroom is drawn to a scale of 1:100.

On the plan, the area of the floor is 72 cm². Calculate the actual area

a in square centimetres   **b** in square metres

10 Bushra builds a doll's house to a scale of 1:50. She models it on her own house.

The area of the roof is 100 m².

What is the area of the doll's house roof?

a in square metres

b in square centimetres

11 The area of Cheriton Wood is about 1 km².

What area will this cover on a 1:50 000 Ordnance Survey map?

12 On a 1:50 000 Ordnance Survey map, Winchester covers an area of roughly 70 cm².

Roughly what area does Winchester cover in real life?

13 The Explorer maps for walking or mountain biking use a scale of 1:25 000.

a What distance on the ground does 1 cm on the map represent?

i in metres   **ii** in kilometres

b What area on the ground does 1 cm² on the map represent?

i in square metres   **ii** in square kilometres

c Llyn Peris, the site of a hydroelectric power plant in Snowdonia, covers an area of 8 cm² on the Explorer map.

What area does Llyn Peris cover in reality?

Constructions (2)

- Constructing a triangle given the lengths of all three sides
- Constructing a shape made of triangles

Keywords

You should know

explanation 1a   explanation 1b   explanation 1c   explanation 1d

1 Construct each of these triangles.
Use a ruler and a pair of compasses. Do not use a protractor.

a **i** Triangle PQR
PQ = 6 cm, PR = 6 cm, QR = 6 cm

ii What type of triangle is PQR?

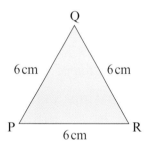

b **i** Triangle XYZ
XY = 4 cm, XZ = 6 cm, YZ = 6 cm

ii What type of triangle is XYZ?

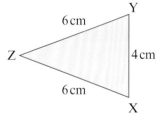

c **i** Triangle ABC
AB = 10 cm, AC = 5 cm, BC = 12 cm

ii What type of triangle is ABC?

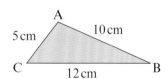

2 Using a ruler and a pair of compasses only, try to construct triangle LMN
where LM = 10 cm, LN = 4 cm and MN = 3 cm.

Is it possible to construct triangle LMN? Explain your answer.

3 The table shows the side lengths of some triangles. Which triangles can be constructed?

Triangle	Dimensions
ABC	AB = 15 cm, AC = 9 cm, BC = 9 cm
DEF	DE = 10 cm, DF = 10 cm, EF = 10 cm
GHI	GH = 20 cm, GI = 9 cm, HI = 7 cm
JKL	JK = 7 cm, JL = 6 cm, KL = 15 cm
MNO	MN = 10 cm, MO = 4 cm, NO = 10 cm

explanation 2a   explanation 2b   explanation 2c

4 Quadrilateral ABCD has these dimensions.

AC = 13 cm   AD = 7 cm

AB = 5 cm   CD = 7 cm

BC = 12 cm

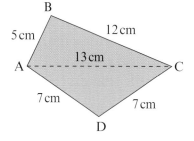

a Using a ruler, draw the line AC.

b Using a pair of compasses, construct the quadrilateral ABCD.

c Measure BD.

5 A kite WXYZ has these dimensions.

WY = 8 cm

WX = 4 cm

XY = 5 cm

a Using a ruler, draw the line WY.

b Using a pair of compasses, construct kite WXYZ.

c Measure XZ.

6 A parallelogram DEFG has these dimensions.

DF = 10 cm   DE = 3 cm   DG = 8 cm

a Using a ruler, draw the diagonal DF.

b Using a pair of compasses, construct parallelogram DEFG.

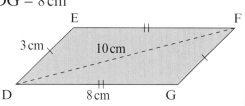

7 The diagram shows a triangular timber roof frame.

Using a ruler and a pair of compasses, construct a diagram of the frame. Use a scale of 1:200.

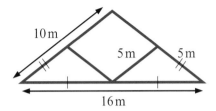

8 The diagram shows a garden EFGH.
EG = 10 m and FH = 7 m

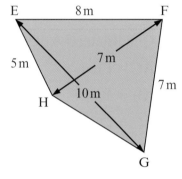

a Using a ruler and a pair of compasses, construct a diagram of the garden. Use a scale of 1:125. Begin by constructing the triangle EFG.

b Measure the length GH on your diagram.

c What is the length GH in the real garden?

9 A garden designer has drawn a patio in the shape of a regular hexagon.

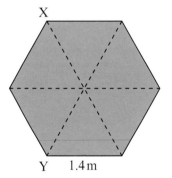

a Using a ruler and a pair of compasses, construct a scale drawing of the patio. Use a scale of 1:35.

b What is the distance XY on the real patio?

10 You can make a model of a regular octahedron by constructing a net made from 8 equilateral triangles.

Construct the net shown on a sheet of A4 card.

The net fits onto A4 card if the length of one side of the equilateral triangle is 7 cm and you place vertex A 7 cm up from the bottom left corner of the card.

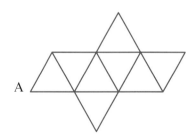

Add tabs where necessary, cut out the net and make it into an octahedron.

11 An octahedron does not have to be regular.
This octahedron is made from 8 triangles
that have sides of 5 cm, 6 cm and 7 cm.
Using a ruler and compasses, draw a net for
this octahedron and make it.

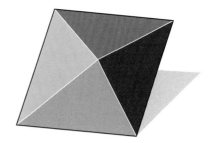

12 A regular tetrahedron is made from 4 equilateral triangles.

Here is a net of a regular tetrahedron.

What happens if the triangles are not equilateral?

Can you always, sometimes or never make a tetrahedron
if the triangles are not equilateral?

Using ruler and compasses, draw nets and test your hypothesis.

13 These formulae give the side lengths, a, b and c, of a triangle in centimetres.

$$a = \frac{n(2m + n)}{2} \qquad b = m(m + n) \qquad c = \frac{(m + n)^2 + m^2}{2}$$

a $m = 1$ and $n = 3$. Find the sides a, b, and c. Construct the triangle.

b Choose three different pairs of whole-number values of m and n.
For each pair, find the sides a, b and c. Construct the triangles.

c What type of triangle do you get each time?

14 a i Construct a triangle with side lengths 6.5 cm, 7 cm and 7.5 cm.

ii Construct a triangle with side lengths 2 cm, 6.5 cm and 7.5 cm.

iii Construct a triangle with side lengths 2.8 cm, 9.1 cm, and 10.5 cm.

b Use your answers to part **a** to help explain why the following information
is not enough to describe triangle ABC completely.

AB = 7.5 cm   AC = 6.5 cm   ∠ABC = 53°

c Use your answers to part **a** to help explain why the following information
is not enough to describe triangle DEF completely.

∠DEF = 113°   ∠EFD = 53°   ∠EDF = 14°

Loci

- Constructing the locus of points from a fixed point
- Knowing when to use solid or dashed lines in locus diagrams
- Constructing the locus of points equidistant from two fixed points or two fixed lines
- Constructing a regular hexagon
- Constructing the locus of points from a line

Keywords

You should know

explanation 1a   explanation 1b

1 Using a pair of compasses, construct the locus of all the points 5 cm from a point X.

2 Using a pair of compasses, construct the locus of all the points no more than 3 cm from a point O.

3 Construct the locus of all the points at least 2 cm, but less than 5 cm, from a point A. Use a pair of compasses.

4 Using a ruler, draw a rectangle ABCD so that AB = 4 cm and AD = 7 cm as shown.

Shade the locus of all the points in the rectangle that are at least 3 cm from A and C.

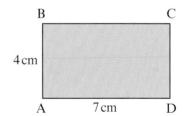

5 Using a ruler, draw a rectangle PQRS, so that PQ = 3 cm and QR = 8 cm.

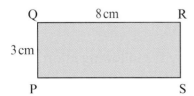

a Mark the midpoint of PS. Label it X.

b Shade the locus of all the points in the rectangle that are more than 2 cm from X and at least 1 cm from both Q and R.

6 You need a pair of compasses and a ruler for this question.

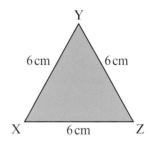

a Construct an equilateral triangle XYZ of side length 6 cm as shown.

b Shade the region within the triangle that is at least 3 cm from X, Y and Z.

> explanation 2

7 Copy the diagram onto squared paper. Construct the locus of the points equidistant from P and Q.

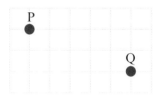

8 Copy the diagram onto squared paper. Shade the locus of the points closer to L than M.

9 The diagram shows triangle ABC.

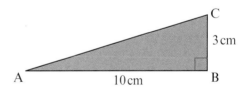

a Copy the diagram. Construct the locus of points equidistant from A and B.

b On the same diagram, construct the locus of points equidistant from A and C.

c What do you notice about the point where both loci intersect?

10 Mark a point O.

a Draw the locus of points 4 cm from O.

b Mark a point A on this locus.

c Construct part of a locus of points 4 cm from A, such that it intersects with the original locus. Label the point of intersection B.

d Using a ruler, draw the lines OA, AB and OB.

e Describe the shape drawn.

11 Use a similar method to that in the previous question to construct a regular hexagon.

explanation 3

12 Lines OA and OB are both 7 cm long and form an angle of 60° as shown.

Copy the diagram and construct the locus of points equidistant from OA and OB.

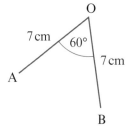

13 A rectangle ABCD has dimensions as shown.

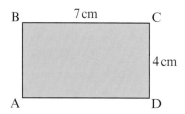

a Using a ruler, copy the diagram.

b Construct the locus of points that are equidistant from edges BA and BC. Mark the point of intersection of the locus with side AD as X.

c Measure the distance XD.

d Construct the locus of points equidistant from BX and BC.

e Mark the point of intersection of this locus with the edge of the rectangle Y.

f Measure the distance YD.

14 A goat is tethered to a post by a rope 9 m long. Draw a diagram of the locus of points in the field that the goat can reach. Use a scale of 1 : 180.

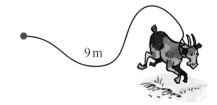

15 A metal rail 4 m long is fixed to a long wall as shown.
A horse is tethered to the rail by a rope 2 m long.
The rope can run freely along the full length of the rail.

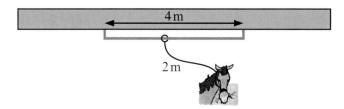

Using a scale of 1 : 100, draw a diagram showing the locus of points that the horse can reach.

16 The diagram shows a courtyard.

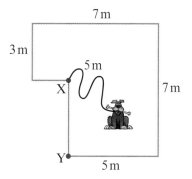

a A dog is tethered to a hook at corner X by a chain 5 m long.

Using a scale of 1 : 100, draw a scale diagram. Shade the locus of all the points that the dog can reach.

b Using a scale of 1 : 100, draw another scale diagram. Shade the locus of all the points that the dog can reach when it is tethered to the hook at corner Y by the same chain.

17 The diagram shows a bare rectangular garden ABCD.
The owner wishes to plant grass in the garden according to these rules.

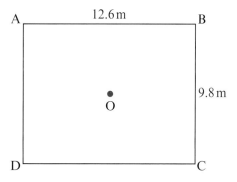

• It must be further than 2.8 m from the tree planted in the centre of the garden at O.

• It must be at least 2.1 m from the edge of the garden.

a Draw a scale diagram of the garden. Use a scale of 1 : 140.

b Shade the locus of all the points where the grass can be planted.

211

18 A river has parallel banks 5.6 m apart. Two points A and B are 7 m apart on the south bank as shown.

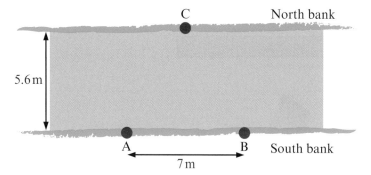

A dog swims across the river to a point C on the north bank, in such a way that he is always equidistant from A and B.

a Draw a scale diagram of the river using a scale of 1 : 140 .

b Using a pair of compasses, construct the locus of points represented by the dog's path across the river.

c By measuring, calculate the real distance of point C from B.

19 Points T and R are 8 km apart.
There is a radio transmitter at T and a receiver at R. The transmitter's range is 6 km (its signal cannot be received more than 6 km from T).

a Make a scale drawing showing the positions of T and R.
Use a scale of 1 : 200 000.

b A relay station at P receives the radio signal from T and re-transmits it to R.

i Explain why the distance PT cannot be more than 6 km.

ii The range of the relay station's transmitter is 4.8 km.
What is the greatest possible distance between P and R?

iii On your diagram, shade the locus of possible positions of P.

c The relay station at P is demolished and a new transmitter is built at a point S. The range of the new transmitter is 10 km.

i The receiver at R must be able to receive signals from S.
What is the greatest allowable distance between R and S?

ii To avoid interference, no point should receive signals from both T and S.
What is the smallest allowable distance between S and T?

iii On your diagram, shade the locus of the possible positions of S.

Bearings

- Measuring and calculating three-figure bearings
- Drawing diagrams involving three-figure bearings

Keywords

You should know

explanation 1a   explanation 1b   explanation 1c   explanation 1d

1 Calculate the three-figure bearing of B from A in each of these diagrams.

a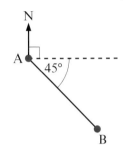

b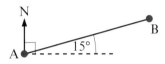

c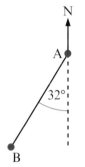

d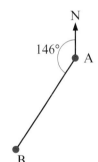

2 Without measuring, calculate the three-figure bearings of A from B in each of the diagrams in question **1** above.

From now on, you will need a protractor. Take North to be vertically up the page.

3 a Copy the diagram on squared paper.

b Showing your construction clearly, measure the bearing of B from A.

c Calculate the bearing of A from B.

d What is the difference between your answers for **b** and **c**?

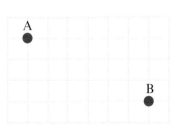

4 a Copy the diagram on squared paper.

b Showing your construction clearly, measure the bearing of Q from P.

c Calculate the bearing of P from Q. Show your working.

d What is the difference between your answers for **b** and **c**?

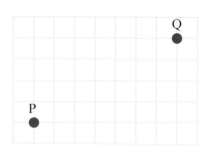

5 a Plot two points, L and M, so that they are 7 cm apart and the bearing of M from L is 020°.

b Calculate the bearing of L from M. Show your working.

c Check your answer to part **b** by measuring.

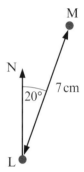

6 a Plot two points, J and K, such that they are 3 cm apart and the bearing of K from J is 322°.

b Calculate the bearing of J from K. Show your working.

c Check your answer to part **b** by measuring.

7 Two points, K and L, are 7.5 km apart. L is due north of K.
A third point, M, is on a bearing of 045° from L and on a bearing of 022° from K.

a Plot the points K, L and M using a scale of 1 : 125 000.
Remember to make a sketch first.

b i Measure the distance of M from both K and L on your diagram.

ii Calculate the actual distance of M from both K and L.

c Without measuring, calculate the angle LMK. Show your working.

d Calculate the bearing of L from M.

8 Town X is 8 km due west of town Y.
A third town Z is on a bearing of 155° from X and on a bearing of 225° from Y.

a Make a scale drawing using a scale of 1 : 100 000. Locate the position of Z.

b **i** To the nearest millimetre, measure the distance of Z from both X and Y.

   ii What is the real distance of Z from X and Y in kilometres?

c Without measuring, calculate the angle YXZ.

d Without measuring, calculate the angle XZY.

9 Points V and W are 60 km apart.
The bearing of W from V is 120°.

a Make a scale drawing showing the position
of V and W. Use a scale of 1 : 750 000.

b Construct the locus of points that are
equidistant from V and W.

c A point U is 45 km from both V and W.
Mark on your diagram the possible positions for point U.

d Measure the bearing of V from each of the possible positions for U.

e Measure the bearing of W from each of the possible positions for U.

10 Town B is 6.50 km due east of Town A.
Town C is 4.55 km from A and on a bearing of 125°.

a Using a scale of 1 : 130 000, draw a scale diagram showing the positions of
the three towns relative to each other.

b Measure the bearing of town B from town C.

c Measure the distance, in centimetres, between B and C on your diagram.

d Calculate the actual distance, in kilometres, between towns B and C.

11 Ahmed, Brian and Carlos are standing in a large field. Carlos is 210 m due
north of Brian. Ahmed is 135 m and on a bearing of 300° from Brian.

a Using a scale of 1 : 3000, draw a scale diagram showing the position of the
three boys relative to each other.

b What is the bearing of Carlos from Ahmed?

c What is the actual distance between Ahmed and Carlos?

12 Lighthouse L is 32.5 km due west of lighthouse M as shown in the diagram.

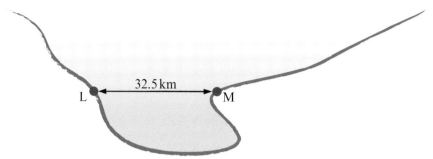

A distress signal is received from a boat, B, out at sea. From L the distress signal is on a bearing of 010°. From M the distress signal is on a bearing 315°.

a Using a scale of 1:500 000, draw a scale diagram showing the position of L and M relative to each other.

b Using a protractor, find the position of the boat B.

c On your diagram measure the distance of the boat from each of the lighthouses, in centimetres.

d Calculate the actual distance, in kilometres, of the boat from each of the lighthouses.

13 Two observers, P and Q, are standing on a shoreline 9 km apart. The bearing of P from Q is 320°.

Boat X is 8.25 km due east of P.

Boat Y is 4.80 km on a bearing of 025° from Q.

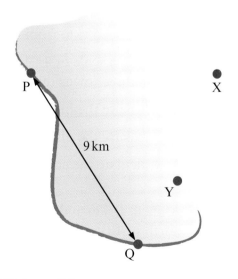

a Using a scale of 1:150 000, draw a scale diagram of the positions of P, Q, X and Y relative to each other.

b Measure the distance XY on your diagram.

c Calculate the actual distance between boats X and Y.

d What is the bearing of X from Y?

e What is the bearing and actual distance of X from Q?

f What is the bearing and actual distance of Y from P?

14   Mayday! Mayday!

The coastguard station gets an SOS message from a sinking trawler.

The message they receive is broken by static and all they hear is

'… buoy A is on a bearing of 300° from us and … B is on … of 027° from us. … sinking fast … SOS SOS …'

Imagine you are the coastguard who receives the message.

Your map shows buoys A and B are 5 km apart and the bearing of B from A is 100°.

Discuss with a partner how you would tackle this before drawing anything accurately.

When you have decided how to tackle it, find where the trawler could be and rescue the crew!

15   Phil, Liz, Charlie, Andi and Ed go on their Duke of Edinburgh weekend expedition, but get lost after leaving their second base (S).

They know they walked at a steady 4 kilometres per hour for 2 hours.

They see the third base (T) on a bearing of 225°.

They know that T was 14 km on a bearing of 200° from S when they set out.

Work with a partner. Draw a diagram to show where they could be and work out the least and most time it will take them to get to T if they walk at the same speed directly towards T.

Collecting data

- Selecting an appropriate class interval for grouping continuous data
- Preparing grouped frequency tables from lists of data

explanation 1a   explanation 1b

1 These are the weights in grams of 24 eggs.

65.3 75.4 59.6 58.7 65.0 57.5 68.2 52.4 74.7 57.4 63.4 52.4

46.7 52.9 76.3 52.5 71.1 48.0 62.4 81.2 53.1 69.8 49.6 50.5

a Copy and complete the grouped frequency table.

Egg weight in grams	Frequency
$43 \leq w < 53$	
$53 \leq w < 63$	
$63 \leq w < 73$	
$73 \leq w < 83$	

b The sizes of eggs in the EU have been defined using the following table.

Size	Mass per egg
Very large	73 g and over
Large	63–73 g
Medium	53–63 g
Small	53 g and under

Describe one difficulty in using this table.

2 These are the times in seconds taken by the 14 finalists at a sports day to sprint 100 m.

12.24	12.36	12.65	13.00	12.50	14.27	13.78
13.02	13.00	13.78	12.92	13.50	13.05	12.56

Copy and complete the grouped frequency table for this set of data.

Time	Frequency
$12.0 \leq t < 12.5$	
$12.5 \leq t < 13.0$	
$13.0 \leq t < 13.5$	
$13.5 \leq t < 14.0$	
$14.0 \leq t < 14.5$	

3 Complete a grouped frequency table for each set of data.

a The hand spans in centimetres of 14 pupils in one class.

Use class intervals of 2 cm for this data.

12.5	9.5	12.0	12.3	18.9	13.5	14.7
15.1	17.6	15.3	15.7	18.1	13.8	16.7

b The height in centimetres of sixteen 11-year-olds.
Use class intervals of 5 cm for this data.

160.91	150.12	159.77	163.02	166.79	162.49	152.89	159.31
152.31	160.55	151.46	152.07	148.08	173.88	152.90	158.63

c The weight in milligrams of twelve 10 mg tablets.

10.043	9.945	9.976	10.029	9.874	9.995
10.015	10.056	9.917	10.082	9.989	9.965

4 Here are the birth weights in grams of 16 pupils.

3340	3780	2450	3780	3400	940	3050	3590
4020	3640	3670	3540	3450	1500	3540	3340

a Complete a grouped frequency table for these weights.

b A baby who weighs less than 2500 g at birth is classified as having a low birth weight.
What percentage of the pupils had a low birth weight?
Give your answer to 1 decimal place.

5 This table shows the median household income in dollars for 25 states in the US in 2005.

a Construct a grouped frequency table for household income in the United States in 2005.

b Approximately what percentage of households earn less than the median salary in each state?

c Why does the table give the median salary in each state rather than the mean salary?

State	Income ($)
Alabama	36,936
Arizona	44,402
Arkansas	35,041
California	53,627
Hawaii	56,133
Idaho	41,269
Indiana	44,051
Kansas	42,861
Kentucky	37,377
Louisiana	36,547
Massachusetts	57,176
Michigan	46,072
Minnesota	52,048
Mississippi	33,090
New Jersey	61,694
New York	49,365
North Carolina	40,781
North Dakota	40,818
Oklahoma	37,020
Pennsylvania	44,545
Tennessee	38,947
Texas	42,165
Utah	48,155
Washington	49,372
West Virginia	33,466

Analysing data (2)

- Estimating the mean of grouped continuous data
- Identifying the modal class of grouped data
- Realising that the mean of grouped data is often very close to the mean of the raw data

Keywords

You should know

explanation 1a   explanation 1b

1 This table shows the heights of one hundred 12–14-year-old pupils.

   a Calculate the estimated mean height. Give your answer to 1 decimal place.

   b What is the modal class?

Height (cm)	Frequency
$130 \leq h < 140$	2
$140 \leq h < 150$	12
$150 \leq h < 160$	35
$160 \leq h < 170$	42
$170 \leq h < 180$	5
$180 \leq h < 190$	4

2 The grouped frequency table is based on a government census and shows how long it takes people to get to work.

   a Calculate the estimated mean time to get to work in minutes.

   b Explain why it is only possible to calculate an estimated mean from this table.

   c How many workers spent 35 minutes or more travelling to work each day?

   d What is the modal class?

   e Approximately what percentage of the population work between 15 and 20 minutes from home?

Time (minutes)	Frequency (millions)
$0 \leq t < 5$	4
$5 \leq t < 10$	14
$10 \leq t < 15$	18
$15 \leq t < 20$	19
$20 \leq t < 25$	16
$25 \leq t < 30$	6
$30 \leq t < 35$	14
$35 \leq t < 40$	3
$40 \leq t < 45$	3
$45 \leq t < 60$	7

3 Taylor and Tilly are growing Scarlet Sprinter runner beans on their allotment.
The seed packet claims 'the smooth straight pods average 38 cm in length'.
The girls measure 25 beans and record the result in a grouped frequency table.
Use the table to comment on the packet's claim.
Give possible reasons for any difference in the results.

Length (cm)	Frequency
$30 \leq l < 32$	1
$32 \leq l < 34$	1
$34 \leq l < 36$	2
$36 \leq l < 38$	5
$38 \leq l < 40$	6
$40 \leq l < 42$	5
$42 \leq l < 44$	4
$44 \leq l < 46$	1

4 These are the prices of 20 houses for sale on an estate.

£146 000	£135 000	£123 950	£159 000	£145 000
£135 000	£146 500	£165 000	£157 500	£123 500
£153 000	£156 000	£132 750	£158 000	£136 000
£149 000	£146 250	£167 500	£148 950	£149 500

  a Calculate the mean house price.

  b Calculate the range of the house prices.

  c Construct a grouped frequency table for this data.

  d Use your table to calculate an estimate of the mean of the house prices.

  e Compare the mean obtained from the grouped and ungrouped data.

  f What do you notice about the mode and the modal class?
Which represents the data better?

5 The grouped frequency diagram shows the lengths of 40 snakes at a snake farm.

The scale is missing from the axis showing the frequency.
You will need to use the table to work out what the values should be.

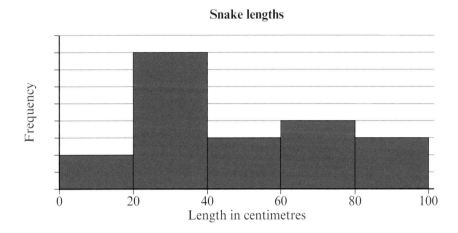

Snake lengths

a Copy and complete this grouped frequency table.

Length (centimetres)	Frequency
$0 \leq L < 20$	
$20 \leq L < 40$	
$40 \leq L < 60$	6
$60 \leq L < 80$	
$80 \leq L < 100$	

b What is the modal group?

c Estimate the mean length of these snakes.

d What percentage of snakes are more than 40 cm but less than 80 cm long?

e Two new identical snakes are bought in and the estimate of the mean length of the snakes changes to 50 cm.
In which class interval will the length of these new snakes go?
Show your working.

6 Sam lives in Cambridge.
One summer he decides to visit 15 of his friends in different cities around the UK.
The cities and their distances by road from Cambridge are given in the table. The distances to City X and City Y are missing.
City Y is 200 miles further from Cambridge than City X.

City	Distance from Cambridge (km)
London	98
Portsmouth	216
City X	x
Manchester	258
Sheffield	197
Glasgow	566
Nottingham	139
Liverpool	309
Newcastle-upon-Tyne	369
City Y	y
Exeter	401
Perth	599
Birmingham	155
Leeds	237
Blackpool	366

a   The mean distance of all the cities from Cambridge is 318 km.
Use this average to find the how far City X and City Y are from Cambridge.
Show your working.

b   Construct an appropriate grouped frequency table for this data.

c   Use your grouped data to find these distances.

  i   The estimated mean distance from Cambridge.

  ii The modal group.

d   Compare the averages for the grouped and ungrouped data.

7 These are the lengths in minutes and seconds of the tracks on two of Ben's CDs.

4:54	5:19	4:17	4:58	2:50	4:25
4:45	4:10	1:30	3:47	4:52	4:54
4:16	3:21	5:07	4:31	4:54	3:55
2:36	3:44	4:25	1:58	5:00	4:55

a **i** Find the mean track length in minutes and seconds to the nearest second.

ii Find the range of the track lengths in minutes and seconds.

b Copy and complete the grouped frequency table.

Time (minutes)	Frequency (millions)
$1{:}30 \leq t < 2{:}00$	
$2{:}00 \leq t < 2{:}30$	
$2{:}30 \leq t < 3{:}00$	
$3{:}00 \leq t < 3{:}30$	
$3{:}30 \leq t < 4{:}00$	
$4{:}00 \leq t < 4{:}30$	
$4{:}30 \leq t < 5{:}00$	
$5{:}00 \leq t < 5{:}30$	

c Use the table to find these times.
Give your answer in minutes and seconds to the nearest second.

i The estimated mean track length.

ii The modal class.

d Compare the mean and the mode or modal class obtained from the grouped and ungrouped data.

Comparing distributions

- Interpreting more complex graphs
- Giving possible reasons for the shapes of graphs
- Justifying explanations using the evidence from calculations

Keywords

You should know

explanation 1a   explanation 1b

1   Two types of battery were tested to compare how long they last.
    30 batteries of each type were tested under the same conditions.
    The results are shown in the tables.

Battery type A	
Duration (hours)	Frequency
$0 \leq t < 5$	2
$5 \leq t < 10$	4
$10 \leq t < 15$	5
$15 \leq t < 20$	6
$20 \leq t < 25$	4
$25 \leq t < 30$	5
$30 \leq t < 35$	4

Battery type B	
Duration (hours)	Frequency
$0 \leq t < 5$	0
$5 \leq t < 10$	0
$10 \leq t < 15$	12
$15 \leq t < 20$	13
$20 \leq t < 25$	4
$25 \leq t < 30$	1
$30 \leq t < 35$	0

$0 \leq t < 5$ means that the duration includes
0 and goes up to but does *not* include 5.

a   Draw a grouped frequency diagram for the results of each type of battery.

b   Calculate an estimate for the mean duration of each type of battery.

c   Which battery type is more reliable? Justify your answer.

d   A youth group is doing a sponsored 24-hour dance.
    They need to choose the batteries that are most likely to last the full 24 hours.
    Which battery type should they choose? Justify your answer.

2 The age distribution of the population in two countries is shown below.
The distribution is given as a percentage for each age group.

Country A	
Age (years)	**Percentage**
$0 \leq A < 20$	24
$20 \leq A < 40$	30
$40 \leq A < 60$	28
$60 \leq A < 80$	14
$80 \leq A < 100$	4

Country B	
Age (years)	**Percentage**
$0 \leq A < 20$	40
$20 \leq A < 40$	28
$40 \leq A < 60$	19
$60 \leq A < 80$	10
$80 \leq A < 100$	3

a Draw a grouped frequency diagram for each country.

b Calculate an estimate for the mean age of the population of country A.

c Calculate an estimate for the mean age of the population of country B.

d Describe in your own words the difference in the age distributions between the two countries.

e One of the countries is from the developed world and one is from the developing world.
Which country is likely to be from the developing world?

f Justify your answer to part **e**.

3 The table shows the temperature at noon every second day in two holiday resorts, A and B, during the month of August.
One resort is in England, the other is in Portugal.

Day	1	3	5	7	9	11	13	15	17	19	21	23	25	27	29	31
Noon temperature (°C) Resort A	32	31	28	34	29	27	31	30	35	31	31	27	32	31	36	30
Noon temperature (°C) Resort B	24	24	31	24	21	22	26	25	32	25	25	24	26	28	19	19

a On the same axes draw line graphs to show the temperatures at noon in the two resorts during August.

b For each resort calculate these statistics.

  i the mean daily midday temperature

  ii the median daily midday temperature

  iii the modal midday temperature

  iv the range in the midday temperatures

c By referring to the line graphs and your calculations in part **b** state, with reasons, which of the resorts is likely to be the one in England.

4 This graph shows the mean house price in different regions of the UK from 1999 to 2007.

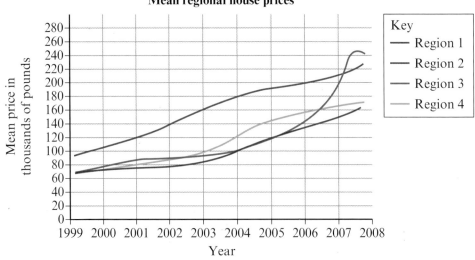

Mean regional house prices

Comment on any similarities and differences in mean house prices in the four regions since 1999.